CW00407001

QUESTIONS ON WITTGENSTEIN

QUESTIONS ON WITTGENSTEIN

RUDOLF HALLER

ROUTLEDGE

First published in 1988 by
Routledge
a division of Routledge, Chapman and Hall
11 New Fetter Lane, London EC4P 4EE
Published simultaneously in the United States
by the University of Nebraska Press

© 1988 Rudolf Haller

Printed in Great Britain

All rights reserved. No part of this book may be
reprinted or reproduced or utilized in any form or
by any electronic, mechanical, or other means, now
known or hereafter invented, including photocopying
and recording, or in any information storage or
retrieval system, without permission in writing from
the publishers.

British Library Cataloguing in Publication Data

Haller, Rudolf
    Questions on Wittgenstein.
    I. Wittgenstein, Ludwig
    I. Title
    192   B3376.W564

    ISBN 0-415-00299-0

Typeset in Times Roman by Leaper & Gard Ltd, Bristol, England

Printed and bound in Great Britain by
Biddles Ltd, Guildford and King's Lynn

Contents

Preface

The present volume contains a selection of nine articles which primarily address questions on Wittgenstein. Although some of them were conceived or completed as much as a decade ago, they appear here essentially unchanged, reflecting the path along which my engagement in Wittgenstein's work has taken me, as well as the current state of Wittgenstein scholarship in Austria and Germany.

I shall not deny that I would have preferred to wait another few years before presenting these questions on Wittgenstein to those of the English-speaking world who might be interested. My hesitation is due to the fact that a further set of questions, unduly neglected in the literature until now, have impressed themselves upon me as worthy of immediate attention. Among the historically interesting questions are those of the nature of Boltzmann's influence upon Wittgenstein, the unique relationship between Karl Kraus and the Viennese philosopher, and (perhaps most importantly) the nature of Piero Sraffa's contribution to the development of the *Philosophical remarks.* The frequent claim that criticism of the position in the *Tractatus logico-philosophicus* on the isomorphic picture has been answered by a Neapolitan gesture only shows how insecure our stance may become when we seek a better position. Questions concerning Wittgenstein's own philosophical position are even weightier: the question of his estimation of the status of philosophical propositions, and that of the disappearance of philosophical problems. Finally, the background of his philosophy of psychology remains largely a riddle to us. Who or what inspired him to attempt the 'classification of psychological phenomena'? What is the purpose of the second part of the *Philosophical investigations*? What role is played by Russell's philosophy of mind, and his later works? Enough has been said to make clear that I see that my own path and that of Wittgenstein scholarship have led to a mountain of unresolved, and to some extent unfamiliar, issues; a mountain shrouded in mist. This picture may seem oddly out of place in the context of the discussion of a philosopher whose sole end in philosophy was to achieve clarity and perspicuity on the philosophical question and its answer.

It was Stuart Shanker who expressed the publisher's wish —

who indeed insisted — that I have a volume of my works on Wittgenstein translated into English. I owe him my gratitude, therefore, for putting my initial doubts to rest. I thank the translator of Chapters 3 through 9, Jane Braaten, for delivering thoughts woven in complex Germanic constructions into what I judge to be a readable English. The original articles — with the exception of Chapter 6 — are published together in two volumes of my edition, *Studien zur oesterreichischen Philosophie*, as Volume 1 (1979) and Volume 10 (1986). The latter volume carries the same title as the present volume. For the transfer of rights, I thank my Dutch editor, Fred van der Zee, as sincerely as I thank Philosophia-Verlag, München-Wien, for permission to reprint Chapter 1, which appears in English in *Austrian philosophy: texts and studies*, edited by J.C. Nyiri, and translated by Barry Smith. I am grateful to Mrs Hilla Hueber and Mr Barry Smith for their help.

As always, special thanks are due to Mrs Helga Michelitsch, whose help was indispensable to the preparation of the work and the typescripts, and who attended to the bibliography. I thank my wife for her careful work on a rainy holiday in Cortina (and, unfortunately, also during the sunny spells) revising with me all the chapters of the book, thereby helping me to avoid several obscurities.

I hope that not too many of these obscurities remain in the *Questions on Wittgenstein.*

R.H.
Universität Graz

Abbreviations

NB   *Notebooks 1914-1916*, ed. G.E.M. Anscombe and G.H. von Wright, trans. G.E.M. Anscombe (Basil Blackwell, Oxford, 1961).

TLP   *Tractatus logico-philosophicus*, trans. D.F. Pears and B.F. McGuinness (Atlantic Highlands, NY: Humanities Press, Inc., 1974).

PI   *Philosophical investigations*, ed. G.E.M. Anscombe and R. Rhees, trans. G.E.M. Anscombe (Macmillan Publishing Co., 1958).

RFM   *Remarks on the foundations of mathematics*, ed. G.H. von Wright, R. Rhees and G.E.M. Anscombe, trans. G.E.M. Anscombe, (MIT Press, Cambridge, Mass., 1983).

BB   *The blue and brown books*, ed. R. Rhees (Harper and Row, NY, 1958).

LA   *Lectures and conversations on aesthetics, psychology and religious belief*, ed. C. Barrett (University of California Press, 1967).

Z   *Zettel*, ed. G.E.M. Anscombe and G.H. von Wright, trans. G.E.M. Anscombe (University of California Press, 1970).

OC   *On certainty*, ed. G.E.M. Anscombe and G.H. von Wright (Basil Blackwell, Oxford, 1969).

PG   *Philosophical grammar*, ed. R. Rhees, trans. A. Kenny (Oxford University Press, Oxford, 1969).

CV   *Culture and value*, ed. G.H. von Wright, trans. P. Winch (University of Chicago Press, 1980; first published as *Vermischte Bermerkungen*, ed. G.H. von Wright (Frankfurt a.m.: Suhrkamp Verlag, 1977).

1

Wittgenstein and Austrian Philosophy

Philosophical schools frequently arise in the emulation or imitation of a teacher whose power of conviction lies in his having asked new questions and often also in his having found or invented an adequate response to new methods of arguing. He succeeds in carrying over paradigm cases of such methods — to labour a theme of T.S. Kuhn — into the phase of normal science wherein their fundamental theoretical and methodological content will not be modified or called into question in any principal way. Modifications which manage to suggest themselves nonetheless are thereafter justified by appeal to the previously acknowledged authorities. And this is not so remarkable if one takes the view that from time immemorial mankind has found it easier to take on new ideas if these come to him in the guise of tradition, than in the awareness of a total break with existing forms of thought.

For this reason also philosophical currents deviating from familiar traditions, either by modifying them or even by seeking to bring them to an end, attempt to legitimate themselves through some tradition or other. And there is indeed a rational basis for this kind of search for historical justification, which may be seen in the empirical need for a *cognitive tradition*. Without such a tradition scientific research would be consigned to an eternally Sisyphean task, since it would repeatedly have to begin again from the start, with no recollection of its past.

The investigation of a school-tradition reduces in the end to the simple problem of giving a genetic account of a phenomenon of the history of ideas: ideas which determine present-day thinking. But let us turn from the question of historical legitimation back to the problem of our own time. Even if we are aware that

1

no claims as to the truth of ideas can be derived from genetic considerations, still they occasionally help us to achieve a shift of the aspect in which thoughts, arguments and theories are experienced.

It is just such a shift of aspect that I treat in this present contribution to the history of the Brentano School, a movement which both initiated and defined the history of Austrian philosophy. It is against its background that one must understand the Vienna Circle, as I have already tried to show elsewhere.[1] That Wittgenstein is to be understood exclusively from this perspective, as some would argue (perhaps overstating their case), would yield a too one-sided picture of this great thinker. But that it is impossible to evaluate him adequately without this perspective seems to me of little doubt.

It is not my aim here however to investigate the genesis of Wittgenstein's thought and the evolution of the Vienna Circle. I wish instead to defend two theses: first, that in the last 100 years there has taken place an independent development of a specifically *Austrian philosophy*, opposed to the philosophical currents of the remainder of the German-speaking world; and secondly that this development can sustain a genetic model which permits us to affirm an intrinsic homogeneity of Austrian philosophy up to the Vienna Circle and its descendants. In the treatment of such a topic a certain limitation is necessary, as also is a statement of the presupposition under which the thesis, which must naturally have the status of a hypothesis, is valid. This presupposition consists in the conviction that if they are to be influential and effective, philosophical ideas, like those of other disciplines, stand in need of institutionalisation. For many centuries the institutions of schools and universities formed the proper (most recently in fact the only) realm of historical influence, not only for this, the oldest of sciences, but indeed for practically all disciplines. It is only against this background that a continuous history of the republic of letters, whose geographical location is the totality of universities and their surrogates — academic chambers, editorial offices, salons — that an explanation of philosophical ideologies and of fashions in philosophical literature becomes possible. But then, precisely because institutions also act as a stabilising force, such that within them the winds of intellectual change blow less strongly than elsewhere, schools and higher institutes of learning not infrequently become the refuge of old and out-dated, petrified theories and traditions. What the obsolete and petrified taste of an established audience signifies for the daring and spirit of an artist protesting against traditional forms and contents, namely an icy lack of understanding or an angry resistance, is not infrequently proffered by the republic of scholars and by institutes of learning to completely 'new' scientific ideas and theories. The history of the arts, as of the sciences, is to a large extent nothing but a collection of examples of this relationship.

So much for presuppositions. As far as limitation is concerned, I shall, in what follows, limit myself only to certain especially important philosophers, without thereby wishing to deny that others could have been included besides those here mentioned, nor to suggest that only 'important' philosophers may have historical influences which are worthy of discussion.

The birth of Austrian philosophy can be seen to lie in the appearance of the *Psychology from an empirical standpoint* in the year 1874. In the same year its author, Franz Brentano (1838-1917), nephew of the romantic poet Clemens, and elder brother of the famous economist and politician Lujo Brentano, was called to the University of Vienna. In what respect can the *Psychology from an empirical standpoint* be conceived as signifying the *terminus a quo* of an independently Austrian development of philosophy? In what respect can a philosopher who attaches himself to Aristotle and recognises himself as his first master serve as forefather to champions of neopositivism who were to inscribe upon their banner the call of death to metaphysics? Can Brentano really belong here to the same extent as, say, the early positivist Ernst Mach? In the answer to this question we can anticipate a significant contribution to the solution of the problem in hand.[2] And the answer is at bottom a simple one, for Brentano's philosophical programme was announced already in the fourth thesis of his *Habilitation* (1866): '*Vera philosophiae methodus nulla alia nisi scientiae naturalis est*' ('The true method of philosophy is none other than that of the natural sciences'). This involves a two-fold claim: first, that the separation of an empirical and a transcendental method proposed by Kant was to be revoked, in favour of the former; and secondly that with the bringing to end of the methodological separation, as for example within the hermeneutic tradition from Dilthey onward, scientific standards — in the strict sense of the natural sciences — should at all events be retained.

In *Psychology from an empirical standpoint* the epistemological foundation of an empirical psychology is laid down. In particular, a *criterion* is sought which would fix the distinction between psychical and physical. This criterion is that of *intentionality*. It asserts that we never conceive, judge, love or hate without conceiving *something*, judging *something*, loving or hating *something*. In short, that all psychical goings on are directed towards objects and that in their possession of this property psychical acts are distinguished from everything physical. In the words of Chisholm, a contemporary interpreter of Brentano, 'we can desire or think about horses that don't exist, but we can ride on only those that do'.[3] In other words, whilst intentional objects do not imply existent objects, intentional acts, like propositional attitudes, do imply intentional objects. Accordingly Brentano modifies also the traditional classification of the psychical acts of thinking, feeling, and willing, and proposes instead presentation and judgement as two fundamentally separate types of thinking, whilst the emotional acts of feeling and willing are not fundamentally distinguished from each other to the same extent, and are indeed conceived together in a single class of emotional acts. What distinguishes the methodology of Brentano and makes it capable of further development is the 'research rule' (F. Hillebrand), or — as one would say today — the 'research programme' (I. Lakatos), which underlies it. The injunctions commanded by this rule fall essentially into three: first, *discipline*; secondly, to carry out one's research empirically and thus to conceive also the evidence of inner perception as a basic kind of fact-perception; thus, it is a consequence of this rule, according to the later Brentano, that the only mode of existence is that of real things. Thirdly the research rule enjoins the application of critical and analytical methods to *language* as a means of discovering and removing fictions and pseudo-problems from philosophy.

Granted that the Kantian tradition of speculative philosophy, too, was concerned to proceed scientifically, and granted also that Kant himself, like his successors, wished to warrant experience in that they investigated the conditions of its possibility, still there are two essential differences which can be made out from even a superficial comparison of the two traditions. Kant's Copernican Revolution — that is, the derivation of the laws of nature from the laws of human understanding, of a transcendental subject — was a philosophical revolution which was *not* undergone by Austrian philosophers. Austrian philosophy is largely characterised indeed, in opposition to all transcendental and idealistic tendencies, by its *realistic* line.

This realism had already *before* the appearance of descriptive psychology attained an influence in the Austria of that time, in the form of Herbartianism and above all in the logical realism of the great Bernard Bolzano. Both Johann Friedrich Herbart (1776-1841) and Bernard Bolzano (1781-1848) had been able to exert, through their students and especially in the mark which they made upon the method of teaching philosophy, a lasting influence upon the formation of the philosophical consciousness of the Austrian school. Herbart had inferred his realist theory of a world of subject-independent atoms from the impossibility of any coherent idealistic alternative, and had perceived the property of objecthood as inhering in concepts, which for him formed the exclusive objects of knowledge. But for Herbart who, like Bolzano, saw himself as belonging to the pre-Kantian tradition of Leibniz, these objects of knowledge must first be legitimised through critical analyses.

In the same way Bolzano, the important theorist and *Vormärz* social revolutionary thinker, presents his thought as standing in sharp opposition to Kant and the German idealists. He reveals his realism not only in that the does not interpret the opposition between the sensible and intelligible world in a subjective idealist way and in that he could regard time and space 'by no means as forms of our sensibility', but above all in his having laid the groundwork of *logical* realism. This is presented in his *Theory of science* (1837) which puts forward a conception of ideas and propositions in themselves resting on an account of meaning as an object independent of thought and speech, something which merits Bolzano's title as grandfather of the modern foundation of logic.[4] The modern conception of logical objects as this burst forth, on the one hand in the work of Gottlob Frege, the most important logician of recent times and, on the other hand, in the triumph over psychologism in logic achieved in Edmund Husserl's *Logical investigations* (1900), is to be found in full clarity in Bolzano's writings.

Thus it is not at all surprising that the work of this great thinker should have received a great deal of attention in the Brentano School, their appreciation of it having been further facilitated through Robert Zimmermann, a student of Bolzano who also taught in Vienna.

This will suffice as to the first of the essential differences. The second, as already stated, is a matter of *methodology*, since neither the method of 'transcendental reductions', nor that of 'synthetic constructions' gained admittance within the tradition of Austrian philosophy. Much more have investigations there been guided by the so-called inductive method of the natural sciences and by the methods of analysis and criticism of language. Thus while Kant and those who have followed in his wake seem largely to have ignored the problem of language, the philosophers of the Brentano School have, like the English empiricists (and indeed under their influence, particularly that of J.S. Mill), brought the necessity of an investigation of linguistic conditions into the very centre of their interests.

Brentano began, as we have stated, with the work of Aristotle. The modes of thought of linguistic analysis had been known and indeed familiar to him ever since his dissertation *On the manifold sense of being in Aristotle.* And of course the same line is revealed also in his concern with the works of J.S. Mill (1806-1873), whose *Logic* had an effect upon the philosophical community of the nineteenth century to an extent which even today has still not been adequately investigated. Whilst the idealistic philosophies influential in Germany had to infer the existence of a problem of language — the problem of the constitutive function of language for thought and for social interaction — largely from the pamphlets of their opponents, Austrian philosophy had, from the very beginning, been characterised, if not always by a tendency towards the *analysis* of language, still by an orientation towards its *criticism.*

After this short characterisation of its differences from the Kantian tradition it seems now to be appropriate to follow the historical currents which mark the rapid establishment of Brentano's students in the universities of the old monarchy. Thus Anton Marty (1847-1914), the important philosopher of language, was called first of all to the newly-founded University of Czernowitz (1875) and subsequently to Prague (1880), where he remained until his death. Thomas Garrigue Masaryk (1850-1937) was likewise called to Prague in 1886, later becoming the first president of the Czechoslovakian Republic. And also Carl Stumpf, the noted epistemologist and founder of the psychology of music, a student of Brentano from his early Würzburg period, first held a position in the University of Prague. Around Marty there assembled a circle of the most faithful disciples of Brentano, Oskar Kraus (1872-1942) and Alfred Kastil (1874-1950) who were responsible for the Brentano-*Nachlass* after the philosopher's death.

Kasimir Twardowski (1866-1938) was called to Lemberg (Lwow) and founded there the Lemberg-Warsaw School of philosophy. L. Kolakowski indeed designates him as being someone who, whilst not himself a positivist, 'trained and encouraged [his pupils] in the detailed analysis of philosophical language'.[5] His most important pupils include Kasimir Adjukiewicz (1890-1963), Jan Lukasiewicz (1878-1956) and Tadeusz Kotarbinski (b. 1866), philosophers and logicians who, in different ways, have had a fundamental influence upon contemporary analytic philosophy. That 'logical anti-irrationalism' — as the guiding idea of the Polish positivists was called by Adjukiewicz — appeared *independently* of the Vienna Circle is only another corroborating factor as to the intrinsic cohesion of Austrian philosophy from Brentano up to and including the Vienna Circle. It was to some extent inevitable that Brentano students should be called also to Innsbruck and to Graz. Thus in 1896 Franz Hillebrand, who had also attended the lectures of Marty in Prague, received a professorial chair in Innsbruck and was succeeded in 1906 by Alfred Kastil, whom we have already met as one of the students of Marty. In 1882 Alexius Meinong (1853-1920), who had four years earlier habilitated under Brentano, was called to Graz. Like many other Brentano students, Meinong grew up philosophically in the literature of English empiricism, and it was in altercation with Locke, Hume and Mill that he developed his philosophical-psychological theories into the fully worked-out theory of objects, which in its turn found a congenial interpreter and critic in Bertrand Russell.[6] It was through Russell's writings that an interest in Meinong's philosophical logic amongst English analytic philosophers was awakened, until, in the last decade, we have seen what amounts almost to a rediscovery of the great philosopher.[7] As regards Meinong's students we shall here recall only Christian von Ehrenfels (1859-1932), titular father of Gestalt psychology and later professor at Prague, Alois Höfler (1853-1922), likewise in Prague and later Ordinarius for philosophy and pedagogy in Vienna, the psychologist Vittorio Benussi who was called to Padova in 1918, Ernst Mally (1879-1944), Meinong's successor to the chair in Graz, the inventor of deontic logic, and finally Franc Veber (1890-1975), the first philosopher at the newly established Slovenian university in Ljubljana.

Less well-known is the fact that Sigmund Freud was a pupil of Brentano for a number of semesters and indeed that it was through Brentano's mediation that Freud became involved in the translation of the works of J.S. Mill. It was Freud who translated Volume 12 of the German Mill edition. And his interpreters have claimed, especially in regard to his earlier works, that they are able to discern a clear influence both of the intentional act structure and of the Brentanian classification of the phenomena of consciousness.[8]

It is of course impossible in this short space even to hint at the theories of the philosophers here listed, especially as one of the most important pupils of Brentano, Edmund Husserl (1859-1938), has still to be mentioned. Husserl's period of adherence to Brentano, from the *Philosophy of arithmetic* (1891) to the crowning work of this period, the *Logical investigations* (1900/1), can be clearly discerned in his philosophical development. The latter work not only signifies the decisive refutation of logical psychologism; it helped also, through the richness of its analyses in the philosophy of language, in the theory of knowledge, and in ontology (which — like Meinong's early works — spring from Husserl's altercation with the empiricist philosophers, especially Hume and Mill), to bring about a new estimation of the objectivism of Bolzano and of the idea of a philosophical grammar. Finally it is this work alone which properly furnishes the research programme of pure phenomenology (something which had been anticipated in Brentano's descriptive psychology). In contrast to this work, Husserl's later turn to the transcendental foundation of phenomenology, to the method of the transcendental reductions, shows very clearly the passage from realism to idealism — as was distinctly recognised by one of his most important pupils, the Polish philosopher Roman Ingarden (1893-1970) in his controversy with Husserl.

It might be appropriate at this point to recall our remarks concerning the institutionalisation of research. As we have seen, and as we could easily confirm at every stage, academic geography has played an extensive role in determining the historical dispersal of ideas. Whilst in Germany it was the influence of Husserl, and later of Heidegger, which grew, and which remained dominant right up until the '60s of this century, neither the remaining Brentano School, nor the philosophy of the Vienna Circle have been able to establish a foothold in German universities; empiricism just does not seem to flourish in every climate. Thus it will be understandable that the philosophy of the new positivism could be disseminated rather in the lands of the old Habsburg monarchy whilst remaining without any kind of reson-ance — apart from the philosophical island of Berlin — in a Germany which was, as we have said, dominated by transcend-ental philosophy.

It is to this latter development which we must now turn. And at first sight it will perhaps seem absurd, even startling, that it is Brentano's name which appears in advance of an account of the history of neopositivistic philosophy. Is this not a mere ana-chronism? Certainly it would be going too far to want to associate the birth of the Vienna Circle with Brentano, even though there are indirect connections between the two. (Brentano was compelled on the occasion of his marriage with Ida von Lieben in 1880, on legal grounds, to relinquish his chair. And although almost every year thereafter the Faculty of Philosophy in Vienna proposed Brentano *unico voco* for the second chair, the necessary imperial consent was never granted. Nevertheless for fourteen years Brentano lectured at the university as *Privatdozent*(!) with unparalleled success, until, disillusioned, he turned his back on Vienna and settled in Florence.) It was the famous physicist Ernst Mach (1838-1916) who after having earlier held positions in Graz and Prague, was called in Brentano's stead to the second chair, specially established for the study of the history and theory of the inductive sciences. As Kolakowski, author of what is so far the best monograph on the development of positivism, clearly recog-nises, Mach defended a presuppositionless and hence anti-metaphysical positivism, less in the sense of Auguste Comte than in that of David Hume.[9] For Mach immediate experience, which alone sanctions the transition from the natural to the scientific attitude to the world, becomes the sole criterion of knowledge: reduction to that which is experientially given is the exclusive *ratio cognoscendi*. However, the carrier of this perception of the given is not a subject, but a 'constellation of elements', just as bodies and other kinds of wholes are nothing other than phenomenal struc-tures of primary and secondary qualities. The elements them-selves should be regarded as neutral as between the categories of the physical and the psychical. Hence the world is not a totality of sensations, but rather a *structure* of 'functional relationships of elements'. The *self* however — Mach said — is 'unsalvageable'. Hence the task of science consists in nothing other than the fitting of thoughts to facts (i.e. to complexes of elements) *and* the fitting of thoughts to one another (a process which is subject to the law of the economy of thought). Thus here already we find outlined in a certain manner the conception of a unified cognition in both the physical and psychical domains.

But we find that the separation of the natural and moral sciences (*Geisteswissenschaften*) is attacked just as clearly, if with different arguments, by Brentano in his critique of the inaugural lecture of Adolf Exner. In his work *On the future of philosophy*, in which this critique is to be found, Brentano defends once more the unity of knowledge, and the arguments which he turns against the opponents of the unity-thesis have not hitherto been taken into account in the dispute between positivism and hermeneutics, although they can be rediscovered — e.g. in the standard work of E. Nagel[10] — without of course any awareness of Brentano's work. Brentano reveals three clear common factors: first, from the standpoint of the objects in question one cannot dispute that even natural processes also have a historical character; second, methodologically, it is not only mechanics which 'rests on fundamental principles from which particular events are deductively explained', for this may be true also of other disciplines. But also not even all natural sciences proceed in the same manner as mechanics. On the contrary, Brentano says, the practice of the natural sciences reveals to us that we vary our processes according to the particular nature of the objects with which we deal: thus even mathematical analysis cannot play the same role in all fields of research. Finally philosophy is itself no exception, since knowledge is in principle always one, that is unified, knowledge.

Thus such different thinkers as Mach and Brentano reveal a theoretical tendency which later reached its full development in the Vienna Circle and in analytic philosophy. And certain genealogical analogies become still clearer when one investigates the writings on methodology and the philosophy of science of A. Höfler and A. Meinong, philosophers in whose works one can point out not only the verification principle but also the principle of falsification, later brought into the centre of consideration by Karl Popper.

Mach's successor in the Chair of Theory and History of Inductive Sciences was, until his suicide in 1906, Ludwig Boltzmann, the founder of statistical mechanics and realistic methodologist of physical science. After him followed Adolf Stöhr (1855-1919) who became prominent not only as a philosopher of biology but also and above all through his writings on the logic of language. Stöhr was of the conviction that glossomorphy and the production of metaphors were a source of mistakes in thinking and he saw one of the principal tasks of philosophical research as lying in the struggle 'between thoughts in development and prevalent speech-forms' since the forms of human thought are not identical with the forms of speech. Like Mach and Boltzmann, Stöhr too condemned metaphysics in so far as the latter claims to provide knowledge or indeed to be a science at all.

At this point one should not forget Fritz Mauthner (1849-1923) who set out at the beginning of the century to instill fear into language. In his *Contributions to a critique of language* (1901-2) he developed his epistemological nominalism whose foundation, as in the case of Mach, is based upon the sensualistic premise that nothing is in our understanding which does not rest on sensual constituents. More decisive still for Mauthner is the belief that language itself is unsuited to knowledge, despite the fact that it is, at the same time, the latter's mouthpiece. And from this dilemma there is only one escape: *critique* of language. Thus whilst it is certainly true that we order the word catalogue of reality according to the alphabet of our language, Mauthner tells us that 'it would be very unphilosophical to believe in the objectivity of this alphabet'. The familiar call 'Back to Kant' he countered with the demand that 'we must return to Hume, in order to proceed from there further into the sceptical critique of knowledge'.

In the year 1922 Moritz Schlick was called to Vienna as the successor of Adolf Stöhr. Around him there gathered a unique circle of thinkers, including Hans Hahn, Philipp Frank, Otto Neurath, Rudolf Carnap, Herbert Feigl, Kurt Gödel, Theodor Radakovic, Friedrich Waismann, but also Felix Kaufmann, Viktor Kraft, Karl Menger and Edgar Zilsel, to name only the most important, who created a philosophical movement from out of which there issued a philosophical force strong enough to first revolutionise philosophy and then to influence its development for half a century. For the circle of logical empiricists founded by these thinkers established a standard of conceptual analysis and of argument which — whatever view one might otherwise adopt concerning their particular theses — has in large measure determined subsequent philosophical thought, and especially all reflection on scientific research; and this standard is something below which we can now no longer fall.

'The turning-point of philosophy'[11] which Schlick announced consisted firstly in securing for philosophy the claim of being a rigorous science, and this was to be achieved by eliminating those pseudo-problems which have found a home within it and, especially within metaphysics. The means for the overcoming of metaphysics should be provided by the logical analysis of language, whose instrument should be modern logic. To the extent that the questions of traditional philosophy concern factual matters they are to be answered by *empirical* sciences, and to the extent that they go beyond this they lack any *cognitive function*, and must be eliminated from the field of cognition. The basis of the elimination process is the so-called '*criterion*' of *meaningfulness*, according to which a sentence is to be acknowledged as meaningful only when one knows also what makes it true, when one can state how it is verified. Here too it was Hume's idea of immediate sensual knowledge which stood in the background as the basis of cognitions of all other types. Metaphysical utterances had to be counted as senseless solely on the basis of the criterion. With regard to the conception of science the thesis of the methodological unity of all sciences was defended in its full strictness — specifically in that it was believed that it would be possible to create a unified language into which all remaining scientific languages could be translatable. It was the language of physics which was first of all considered as one such language, to which therefore all other languages would have to be reducible.

Indubitably however the most significant influence upon the discussions of the Vienna Circle and upon the development of its fundamental tenets was exerted by Ludwig Wittgenstein.[12] Even in an autobiography composed much later, Carnap, for example, still saw a need to correct the view that the philosophy of the Vienna Circle was actually identical with that of Wittgenstein.[13] The *Tractatus* was indeed read and interpreted, sentence by sentence in the Thursday meetings of the Circle. After becoming personally acquainted with Wittgenstein, Schlick came to stand more and more under the latter's direct influence. And even Carnap admits that — beside Frege and Russel — Wittgenstein, above all thinkers, exerted the strongest of influences upon him. And this was in spite of the fact that the somewhat headstrong Wittgenstein already from the beginning of 1929 had declined further meetings with Carnap and Feigl. Thus whilst Schlick and Waismann stood most strongly under the spell of the author of the *Tractatus logico-philosophicus*, Neurath for his part revealed the most sceptical attitude. Above all Neurath distanced himself critically from Wittgenstein's conception of what can only be *shown* and not said. It was Neurath — if Carnap can be believed — who pointed over and over again to the fact that even language itself is a phenomenon which belongs within the world, rather than something which effects the world from without.

It is an interesting fact that Neurath himself seems to have misled most people working on the history of the Vienna Circle by stressing a uniform picture of its development as well as of its main ideas. Propaganda for the new philosophy was, for him, more important than drawing attention to the differences between his own interpretation of (let's say) protocol sentences and Schlick's view.

Actually ever since 1908 he had defended a strong Duhemian argument in favour of a holistic and historical view of science, which in our time has been defended by Quine. Already in 1908 the book *The aim and structure of physical theory* was translated into German by Friedrich Adler and published with a preface by Ernst Mach. Some years later Philipp Frank translated *L'évolution de la mécanique* (1903) into German. Neurath's main points which he traced back to Duhem were, first, that more than one self-consistent system of hypotheses can satisfy a given set of facts, and second, that any testing of a theory has to do 'with a whole network of concepts and not with concepts that can be isolated'. And when Neurath puts forward his dictum of the sailors who on the open sea must reconstruct their ship — a picture which Quine's frequent quotation has brought to our knowledge — Neurath mentions Duhem as the only source of these ideas. In as far as every proposition in a scientific theory is related to all the other propositions, Neurath thinks we can retain its consistency either by changing the proposition which does not cohere with the system, or by changing the system. There are no sentences preferable in themselves. Hence, whenever we test a theory this test will not have as a result true or false propositions, because — this was Duhem's point — the physicist never subjects an isolated hypothesis to experimental test, but only a whole group of hypotheses — therefore if there appears a disagreement between predictions and facts, the experiment never signifies which of the propositions was to be changed.

Such a view as defended by Neurath clearly contrasts with the *Tractatus* position, which stated that every proposition is a *picture* or *model of reality*. But this was not the only field where the two approaches of Wittgenstein and Neurath differed fundamentally.

I think it would be nearer to the truth to say that their views differed in almost every respect. But Neurath does not say this in public. It is mainly from letters so far unpublished that we may grasp how deep the gap between him and the Wittgensteinian view actually was.

It would lead us too far to point out these differences especially since we have to look first at the Wittgensteinian conceptions which were in fact incorporated into the new positivism.

It is of course not as though the Circle came to be completely affected by the theories of Wittgenstein: but of the ideas which were essential to them perhaps the most essential derived from this source and from the influence which Wittgenstein, from the very beginning, and to an increasing extent thereafter, exerted upon the Circle. As Herbert Feigl writes,[14] the main themes of discussion were the foundations of logic and mathematics as well as the logic of empirical knowledge. And the Wittgensteinian conception was not only central for both these topics, it offered in addition a solution which made possible the fundamental differentiation of the new positivism from the old variety. In what did this conception consist? Now it would naturally take us too far afield here to attempt even a sketch of Wittgenstein's theories. It will be necessary to limit ourselves only to that which is absolutely necessary.

The three basic conceptions which were taken over from Wittgenstein by this new positivism were:

(1) its interpretation of logic and of logical propositions,

(2) its theory of empirical propositions,

and finally and above all,

(3) its definition of philosophy.

Ad (1): In accordance with the view expressed in the *Tractatus*, the truth of logical statements consists in their structure alone. They are statements which are true in all possible circumstances, which are — as Leibniz had said — true in all possible worlds. 'It is the peculiar mark of logical propositions that one can recognize that they are true from the symbol alone, and this fact contains in itself the whole philosophy of logic' (TLP 6.113). 'The proposi-

tions of logic are tautologies' (TLP 6.1). 'Therefore the propositions of logic say nothing' (TLP 6.11). Hence logical propositions
cannot be refuted by any possible experience and cannot therefore be confirmed either. In opposition to the account of *a priori*
propositions given by Kant, Wittgenstein denies that the mark of
the logical proposition should be its *generality* or *general validity*. It
is only *necessity* which determines a tautology and every tautology
itself *shows* that it is a tautology (TLP 6.127). 'Outside logic,
everything is accidental', and hence there are no *empirical*, but
only *logical* impossibilities. The truth of logical propositions does
not reveal any connection to the world, as does, say, the truth of
non-analytical propositions, which rests on the accidental existence of factual constellations. In consequence all tautologous
(always true) propositions and all contradictory (always false)
propositions are without any empirical content.

In accordance with the logicist position, mathematics, too is
then reduced to logic. Equations in mathematics, like the propositions of logic, are pseudo-propositions. One cannot in general
agree with the judgement of R. Kamitz, that logic (including
mathematics) fulfils no independent function in the eyes of the
neopositivists.[15] It is true that as a result of the acceptance of the
Wittgensteinian conception, logical propositions are seen as
having *no empirical content*, but they do have a structure, of such a
type that the limits of my language are also the limits of logic.
Logic can certainly not foresee its own application, but it can also
not come into *conflict* with the application of its tautologies.

This theory of the tautological character of logical propositions
leads also to the identification of the latter with the class of *a priori*
propositions and to the *denial* of the possibility of synthetic *a priori*
propositions, the starting point of transcendental reflections.

Ad (2): The neopositivists also took over Wittgenstein's conception of empirical propositions. This is again rooted in their
Humean conviction that everything which we can describe at all
could also have been otherwise. There is no part of our experience which is *a priori* (TLP 5.634). A proposition is empirical then
and only then when one knows and/or when one can state what
makes it true, or would make it true. In order to be able to say
that a surface is white or black one must know what one calls
'white' or 'black', *when* one calls a surface white or black. 'In
order to be able to say, "p" is true (or false), I must have determined in what circumstances I call "p" true, and in so doing I
determine the sense of the proposition' (TLP 4.063).

The working-out of this idea leads to the drawing up of the verification criterion of meaningfulness, that is, of the requirement that it should be possible to state or determine the conditions which would make a sentence true. The problem of the meaning of sentences thereby becomes the central theme of a theory of empirical knowledge and must be distinguished from the problem of confirming that a sentence is true or false.

But what Schlick in fact intended by his demand for verifiability he clearly expresses in the same essay on the turning-point in philosophy. There the demand for the statement of the conditions under which a sentence is true is identified with the statement of the *meaning* of the sentence.[16] Again, the statement of the conditions need not imply that these conditions should be in fact supplied, but Schlick is expressly concerned to show that any *thinkable*, indeed any logically possible verification would be a sufficient criterion for the empirical-cognitive meaningfulness of a sentence. If one were to restrict logical possibilities here to empirical possibilities, then e.g. all statements about past events would have to be meaningless statements.

In a conversation of 22 December 1929 which was led by Wittgenstein in the house of Schlick, Wittgenstein makes some comments regarding his own views concerning verification.[17] He distinguishes two possible conceptions. According to the first, no sentence is completely verifiable, for 'whatever we do we can never be certain that we will not have deluded ourselves'. And the example he employs is: 'Up there on top of the chest there is a book.' Is it sufficient merely to look, Wittgenstein asks, to observe the book from various angles, or must we, in order to verify the sentence, open the book, turn over its leaves, etc.? The sceptic argues that there will always remain open a 'back door'.

Wittgenstein in contrast defends his second conception: 'If I can never completely verify the sentence, then I could have meant nothing by the sentence. But then the sentence says nothing at all.'[18] And Wittgenstein supplements this view with two remarks: first of all that scientific languages fluctuate in the fixing of the meaning of their symbols still less than does everyday language; and secondly — in a conversation conducted three months later[19] — that *also various different* methods of verification can be accepted. From this we can see clearly that Wittgenstein — and with him Schlick — held the belief that the manner of verification depends upon definite conditions, which we determine. Thus in the same essay Schlick says very clearly that 'the sense of a sentence about physical objects is strictly speaking exhausted only by supplying indeterminately many possible verifications, and the consequences of this is that such a sentence can *never* [my emphasis] be shown to be true'. And he goes on: 'it is indeed generally known that even the most certain sentences of science are always to be conceived only as hypotheses, which remain open for further precisation and improvement'.[20] That such hypothetical statements are neither true nor false in the strictest sense was likewise made clear by Wittgenstein in the second of the just-mentioned conversations, through his account of the difference between *statements*, i.e. sentences which have a truth-value, and *hypotheses*. 'A hypothesis', he there tells us, 'is not a statement, but rather a rule for the formation of statements.' And immediately thereafter: 'A law of nature does not admit of verification, nor of falsification. Of a law of nature one can say neither that it is true nor false, but only that it is 'probable', and 'probable' here signifies, simply, comfortable.'[21] Whilst 'physical statements', insofar as they have a predictive character, can never count as having been established, can always come to be discarded or amended, statements with truth-values are, in regard to those truth-values, unalterable. And this says nothing other than that such statements are either true or false.

This view of Wittgenstein's, which was taken over by Schlick and later defended by Ryle, exempts hypothetical propositions from the very beginning from the charge of being meaningless on the basis of the criterion of meaning.

Finally *Ad (3):* The neopositivists accepted Wittgenstein's *conception of philosophy*, which has its core in the view that philosophy is to be interpreted as *critique of language*, and hence also of scientific language. 'Most of the propositions and questions to be found in philosophical works are not false, but nonsensical' (TLP 4.003). Philosophy however advances no theses; it is not a theory, but rather an analysis and uncovering of the surface and deep structure of language. An analysis of this kind is an activity of making clear, of explication: 'philosophy aims at the logical clarification of thoughts' (TLP 4.112). From this the neopositivists derive (1) the name, *logical empiricism*, which they themselves accept, and (2) the definition of their task: elucidation and demarcation of empirical sentences and criticism of all pseudo-propositions. Thus we find also that the demarcation problem is defined in full clarity in Wittgenstein's works, a problem whose discovery is claimed by Popper. 'Philosophy', we are told in TLP

4.113, 'sets limits to the much disputed sphere of natural science', and the latter is for Wittgenstein empirical science *par excellence.*

The criticism and elimination of metaphysics which define the negative part of the programme of logical empiricism make use, like the constructive part, of all three of the main planks of the package of views taken over from Wittgenstein: it rests on an analysis of logical structure and on the employment of the meaning-criterion, and it abstains from advancing any thesis of its own about reality.

Whilst most of the members of the Circle remained faithful to this programme, in the hope that through a purely scientific conception of the world and ultimately through the construction of an axiomatic language of science, the constricting presuppositions of metaphysics might be laid to rest, the mentor of this movement had already taken in hand an extension of the scope of the problems of linguistic analysis.

One of the essential extensions which Wittgenstein undertook is the application of analysis to non-descriptive linguistic utterances of that ordinary, living language, whose logical orderedness had indeed already been affirmed in the *Tractatus.* Thus where he there stated that 'Logic must take care of itself' (TLP 5.473) and in his notebook for 13 October 1914: 'Logic takes care of itself; all we have to do is to look and see how it does it', we are now told that 'Language must speak for itself.'[22] And, as one may add, we need only look and see how it does it. The extension of the subject-matter therefore consists in the following: whilst for the theory of the sentence it is fundamental that the meaning of a name can be determined only in the context of a sentence and is thus dependent upon the sense of the sentence, for the extended theory of language the form of sentences — now no longer merely of categorical affirmative sentences — should be explained in terms of that collectivity of rules which constitute a language. One can call these constitution-rules the *grammar* of a language, and the investigation of these rules a grammatical one. Wittgenstein thus extends the concept of grammar, which normally comprises only the doctrine of the parts of speech and the principles of their combination, in such a way that, as he says, 'What belongs to grammar are all the conditions (the method) necessary for comparing the proposition with reality. That is, all the conditions necessary for the understanding of the sense.'[23] And further:

'Grammar is the account books of language. They must show the actual transactions of language, everything that is not a matter of accompanying sensations.'[24] If all conditions of our understanding belong to the subject-matter of the *grammatica universalis*, then of course one of its principal themes must be the understanding of linguistic utterances. Now is this understanding a process, a mental process, in which that which the speaker intends by his words comes to be grasped, or is it something which must be subjected to some other kind of analysis? The question as to what we are to understand by mental processes at all thus represents just as adequate a statement of our initial problem as the question as to the nature of utterances about our sensations.

The expansion in the formulation of the question naturally also gives rise to reflection upon the methods of the investigation itself, something whose very formulation has constituted a quite special hurdle for most interpreters. For Wittgenstein expressly affirmed that his investigation could only be a *descriptive* one, not one which wants to idealise, i.e. change the phenomenal structure of the objects of investigation. Expressed somewhat pointedly, Wittgenstein holds fast to the rule-governed use of words as this actually takes place within the language, and this he wishes to describe without any theoretical presuppositions. This description is not the general description of a theory, but is quite deliberately a description having a definite purpose, namely 'to remove particular misunderstandings'.[25] 'For the task of philosophy is not to create a new, ideal language, but to clarify the use of our language, the existing language.'[26]

That Wittgenstein turned to the investigation of the use of language does not imply, as might be claimed,[27] the substitution of an *a posteriori* method for an *a priori* one; rather, its basis lay principally in this, that on the one hand the realm of logical syntax became extended, and that on the other hand the problem of meaning was recognised as being eliminable. But this extension of the problem, like that of making unproblematic the difficulties surrounding the notion of meaning, does not serve the purpose of enabling the construction of a theory, much less still of an empirical theory of language; rather are they carried through in the old familiar spirit of the critique of language, they presuppose, that is to say, the same quite special purposes. If it were true that this method was an *a posteriori* (empirical) one, then in any case the intention of extending the realm of empirical data and observation must still be recognisable: thus there would have to

19

be a rapid process of collecting unknown facts which would precede or go in hand with the investigation. Nothing of the like actually takes place. Quite the opposite, since Wittgenstein never becomes tired of emphasising that it is only a matter of setting together what is already known of the arrangement of the phenomena, of seeing correctly or of seeing afresh that with which we are already familiar. 'Our language is in order just as soon as we have understood its syntax and have recognized those of its wheels which are running idle', he states in a conversation with Schlick of 29 December 1929. This image of wheels idling remained for a long period Wittgenstein's metaphor for apparently problematic formations of language which give rise particularly to philosophical confusion. When one reconstructs the syntax of the relevant linguistic system such formations become recognisable as merely spurious. Let us take the frequently used example of an epistemological problem: what holds of objects of perception when they are not being perceived? — 'If I turn myself away does the stove disappear?' — then one is involved here in one typical ploy, that of substituting for the existence-concept appropriate to *empirical* objects another concept, which Wittgenstein calls the metaphysical. According to this interpretation the utterance: 'If I turn myself aways does the stove disappear?' is an idly running wheel.

In the *Tractatus* Wittgenstein had put it thus:

3.327: A sign does not determine a logical form unless it is taken together with its logico-syntactical employment.
3.328: If a sign is useless, it is meaningless. That is the point of Occam's maxim.

If one wants to reconstruct the syntactically correct employment then one has to pay attention to the use of the symbols in the system, in the calculus. This in itself was already a move forward. For according to the *Tractatus* one is not allowed to talk at all in logical syntax of the meaning of the symbols.[28] But if one wants to differentiate between spurious and genuine utterances then one cannot avoid paying attention to meaning, as little as we could in our analysis of the distinction between logically tautologous sentences and materially analytical sentences such as 'No bachelor is a married man.' In my view the majority of interpreters of Wittgenstein have not taken sufficiently seriously the fact which he admitted, that a syntactical or grammatical investigation of meaning is an *investigation having a quite definite purpose*; they applied their attention instead rather to the evolution of Wittgenstein's concept of syntactical system. Not that they thereby asserted something false; but this evolution is more a matter of transformations in the conceptual apparatus of the analysis than a development of its method and content. The method is from the very beginning asserted to be purely descriptive and the content is the grammar of language. Of which language? Well, the language we speak. Granted, this language is a highly complex structure and the tacit agreements which are necessary in order to understand it are — as affirmed in the *Tractatus* — highly complicated. But this cannot relieve us of the task of laying bare those utterances within it which are merely spurious utterances, namely the characteristically philosophical ones. It is *these* which bring about confusion. The problems to which these represent the solutions are not genuine problems, as are the questions posed by the natural sciences, but pseudo-problems, as one can already see in the fact that none of them can be supplied with a generally accepted solution. In many passages, from the *Philosophical remarks* of 1930 up to the *Philosophical investigations* of the forties, Wittgenstein's preferred characterisation for these incriminated philosophical sentences is — as I have already remarked — that of idly running wheels. 'The confusions which occupy us arise when language is like an engine idling, not when it is doing work.'[29] It is therefore confusions called forth through quite specific linguistic forms which characterise philosophical problems. And hence philosophical *criticism*, if it wishes to deal with these problems and dissolve the associated confusions, must first of all investigate, and perhaps reconstruct the system of language; in short it must describe the grammar of the language in which such utterances are formulated. If one conceives language as a structure which has as its basis the description of the world, then Wittgenstein now recognises that we should be justified in talking of a unified structure only if the purpose which it serves were indeed such. But this is not the case: 'Language is not defined for us as an arrangement fulfilling a definite purpose. Rather "language" is for us a name for a collection ...'[30] Thus it is not at all established from the start what the object of linguistic criticism is, the limits of language are not fixed. And this implies that the function of linguistic expressions cannot be seen to lie exclusively in their representative relation to the world, but rather that they have a wide variety of different functions, such that it would be a serious mistake to suppose that these various different functions would allow themselves to be reduced to a single form.

It is also not the case that logic, as the theory of general structures, should have to do with anything other than our language. Already in the *Philosophical remarks* he said on this: 'How strange if logic were concerned with an ideal language and not with *ours*. For what would this ideal language express? Presumably, what we now express in our ordinary language; in this case this is the language logic must investigate. Or something else: but in that case how would I have any idea what that would be? — Logical analysis is the analysis of something we have, not of something we don't have. Therefore it is the analysis of propositions *as they stand*.'[31]

Sentences 'as they are', language 'as it is', are thus the 'rough ground' return to which is demanded by the *Philosophical investigations*. If now the task of philosophy is to consist in the description of ordinary language, does it not thereby renounce one of its most eminent goals, namely the exploration of the essence of the *world*? The *Tractatus* answer to this question in the *Philosophical remarks* shows that even in this matter Wittgenstein did not fundamentally change his opinion. 'What belongs to the essence of the world cannot be expressed by language ... what belongs to the essence of the world simply cannot be *said* ... But the essence of language is a picture of the essence of the world; and philosophy as custodian of grammar can in fact grasp the essence of the world, only not in the propositions of language, but in rules for this language which exclude nonsensical combinations of signs.'[32]

Now in spite of the fact that Neurath and also Frank, Hahn, and Carnap took an opposite line of thinking on the foundations of science to that of Wittgenstein, there are certain stronger affinities which are worth mentioning here.

In connection with the problem of foundation, particularly the epistemic foundation of science, Wittgenstein increasingly adopts a kind of holism similar to the one found in Neurath. However, unlike Neurath, he restricts it to the ultimate basis of our knowledge.

Wittgenstein, when he reflects upon our starting point in building up a *Weltansicht* — a world view — argues that we do not simply learn *rules*, but 'a totality of judgments is made plausible to us' (OC §140).

When we first begin to *believe* anything, what we believe is

not a simple proposition, it is a whole system of propositions. (OC §141)
It is not single axioms that strike me as obvious, it is a
system in which consequences and premises give one
another mutual support. (OC §142)

In various passages of his writings Wittgenstein explains his view
that a whole system of propositions is bound up with our beliefs.
And I regard this view as fundamental for what may be called a
paradigm in T.S. Kuhn's sense, since — although I shall not
enter into this here — it is fundamental for the general mode of
justification that may be given for a certain *Weltansicht*. For example, take our belief that the earth is round, a belief that has
increasingly been confirmed from the voyages of discovery in the
fifteenth century onwards, from Amerigo Vespucci to the age of
artificial satellites:

We know that the earth is round. We have definitively
ascertained that it is round. We shall stick to this opinion.
(OC §291)
Further experiments cannot *give the lie* to our earlier ones, at
most they may change our whole way of looking at things.
(OC §292)

Starting from ideas captured in the remark from Kürnberger
used by Wittgenstein as a motto to the *Tractatus*: 'and anything a
man knows, anything he has not merely heard rumbling and
roaring, can be said in three words', Wittgenstein developed his
philosophy of the sayable and the unsayable, of that which can be
meaningfully said and that *about* which we can only remain
silent. This philosophy of the mystical which was a consequence
of his theory of the sayable was only partially accepted by the
neopositivists. Most of them, like Russell, regarded it with incom-
prehension.

For Wittgenstein himself, an ambivalent neopositivist, the
solution of fundamental scientific questions was not bound up
with the solution of problems of life, not bound up with the question of the meaning of life. For this meaning is something which
could only lie outside the world. 'Ethics does not treat of the
world. Ethics must be a condition of the world, like logic.'
This is the view of the young 27-year-old Wittgenstein, a view

which, if I am right, he never changed, simply because his later philosophy hardly changed at all these fundamental positions of the *Tractatus*.

And in *this* respect the philosophers of the Vienna Circle had after all learned something from the theory of the unsayable, for a scientific ethics was not a constituent part of their scientific conception of the world. 'Scientific reflection', Carnap tells us, 'does not determine the goal but only the pathway to whatever goal has been decided.'[33] Acting practically, in the sense of settling upon a goal, is itself something which can never itself be the result of a theoretical demonstration. All attempts to furnish such questions and answers with an empirical content are useless, since they are the expression merely of feelings, not of thoughts. A principle by means of which our lives are ordered is without doubt thereby deprived of rational control, a consequence which has been made clear only by the later development of the theories of meta-ethics.

I come now to the end of this chapter, in which I have given only a sketch of the development which has led to the present-day situation of philosophy. But what we sometimes seem to forget is the tradition from which these thoughts have issued, a tradition which was still clearly seen by the representatives of the Vienna Circle, especially by Neurath. For in their programmatic writing *The scientific conception of the world: the Vienna Circle* (1929) we find mentioned, beside such familiar empiricists and philosophers of science as Hume and Russell, Mach and Boltzmann, Duhem and Poincaré, also Brentano, Meinong, Höfler and Mally. Thus whoever had believed that neopositivism is to be seen as having sprung exclusively out of developments latent in the old positivism, must accept that its essential postulates, namely (1) the nominalist-Ockhamist principle of the parsimony of principles of explanation, and thus also of existents to which one is committed, (2) the principle of the empirical foundation of all cognition, as well as the principle of the unity of science, belong just as much to the traditional stock-in-trade of Austrian philosophy as do the methods of criticism and analysis of language which led Brentano to his 'renunciation of the non-real'.

It would be very profitable to pursue the history of the influences of these philosophers who have indeed revolutionised the philosophy of our time, even if this radical transformation made itself felt in the land of its birth much later than in other, farther-flung parts of the world. And it would be altogether stimulating to bear in mind also the effects of those philosophers who do not quite fit into the picture outlined here. Neither can be offered here. What I have sought to do is to make clear and to verify, at least in outline, the two theses which I formulated at the beginning. We reserve the possibility that future research may fill out this picture, correct its one-sidednesses and thus provide one building-block for the future history of philosophy which would do justice to the title 'Austrian philosophy'.

Notes

1. R. Haller, 'Meinongs Gegenstandstheorie und Ontologie', *Journal of the History of Philosophy*, 4 (1966), pp. 313-24; R. Haller, 'Ludwig Wittgenstein und die Österreichische Philosophie', *Wissenschaft und Weltbild*, 21 (1968), pp. 77-87; R. Haller, 'Sprachkritik und Philosophie. Wittgenstein und Mauthner', in A. Doppler (ed.), *Die Sprachthematik in der Österreichischen Literatur des 20. Jahrhunderts*, Institüt für Österreich-Kunde (Wien, 1974), pp. 41-56. These papers are now collected in R. Haller, *Studien zur Österreichischen Philosophie* (Rodopi, Amsterdam, 1979).

2. Cf. O. Kraus, *Franz Brentano* (C.H. Beck, München, 1919); A. Kastil, *Die Philosophie Franz Brentanos* (Francke, Bern, 1951).

3. R.M. Chisholm, 'Introduction' to *Realism and the background of phenomenology* (Free Press, Glencoe, 1960), p. 4.

4. Cf. H. Bergmann, *Das philosophische Werk Bernhard Bolzanos* (M. Niemeyer, Halle, 1909); E. Winter, 'Bernhard Bolzano', in *Bernhard Bolzano-Gesamtausgabe* (Stuttgart, 1969) vol. 1; E. Morscher, 'Von Bolzano zu Meinong: Zur Geschichte des logischen Realismus' in R. Haller (ed.), *Jenseits von Sein und Nichtsein* (Akademische Drückü. Verlagsanstalt, Graz, 1972).

5. L. Kolakowski, *The alienation of reason: A history of positivist thought*, trans. N. Guterman (Garden City, NY, 1968).

6. Cf. B. Russell, *Essays in analysis*, ed. D. Lackey (George Allen & Unwin, London, 1973).

7. Cf. *Revue Internationale de Philosophie*, 2-3 (1973); Haller (ed.), *Jenseits von Sein und Nichtsein*; M. Lenoci, *La teoria della con noscenza in Alexius Meinong* (Università Catolica, Milano, 1972); K. Salamun, 'Das philosophische Seminar an der Universität Graz', *Historisches Jahrbuch der Stadt Graz*, 5/6 (1972); see also J.N. Findlay, *Meinong's theory of objects and values*, 2nd edn (Clarendon, Oxford, 1963); R. Grossmann, *Meinong* (Routledge & Kegan Paul, London, 1974).

8. Ernest Jones, 'Das Leben und das Werk von Sigmund Freud', *Journal of the History of Ideas*, 6 (1945); A. Wucherer-Huldenfeld, 'Sigmund Freud als Philosoph', *Wissenschaft und Weltbild*, 21 (1968).

9. Cf. Kolakowski, *The alienation of reason*; R. Kamitz, *Positivismus*

(Langen Müller, München-Wien, 1973).

10. E. Nagel, *The structure of science. Problems in the logic of scientific explanation* (Harcourt, Brace and World, New York, 1961).

11. First published in *Erkenntnis*, 1 (1930), pp. 4-11, repr. in M. Schlick, *Gesammelte Aufsätze 1926-1936* (Wien, 1938).

12. K.T. Fann, *Wittgenstein's conception of philosophy* (Blackwell, Oxford, 1969); A. Janik and S. Toulmin, *Wittgenstein's Vienna* (Simon & Schuster, New York, 1973); cf. Jörgen Jörgensen 'The development of Logical Positivism', *International Encyclopedia of Unified Sciences* (University of Chicago Press, Chicago, 1957), vols 2/9; G. Pitcher, *The philosophy of Wittgenstein* (Prentice Hall, Englewood Cliffs, NJ, 1964); A. Kenny, *Wittgenstein* (Penguin, Harmondsworth, 1973); R. Haller, 'Ludwig Wittgenstein' in W. Pollak (ed.), *Tausend Jahre Österreich. Eine biographische Chronik*, vol. 3 (Jugend und Volk, Wien-Munich, 1974), pp. 317-22.

13. Cf. P.A. Schilpp (ed.), *The philosophy of Rudolf Carnap* (Library of Living Philosophers), (La Salle, Ill. 1963), p. 24.

14. H. Feigl, 'Logical empiricism', in D. Runes (ed.), *Twentieth century philosophy* (New York, 1974), p. 408.

15. Kamitz, *Positivismus*, p. 123.

16. Schlick, 'The turning point in philosophy'.

17. F. Waismann, *Wittgenstein and the Vienna Circle*, ed. B.F. McGuinness (Dordrecht, 1979); trans. J. Schulte and B.F. McGuinness (Basil Blackwell, Oxford, 1979).

18. Ibid.

19. 20 March 1930.

20. Schlick, *Gesammelte Aufsätze*, p. 95.

21. Waismann, *Wittgenstein and the Vienna Circle*, 22 March 1930.

22. L. Wittgenstein, *Philosophische Grammatik*, Schriften 4, p. 40.

23. Ibid., p. 88.

24. Ibid., p. 87.

25. Ibid., p. 115.

26. Ibid.

27. Cf. Fann, *Wittgenstein's conception of philosophy*, p. 43; D. Pears, *Ludwig Wittgenstein* (Fontana, London, 1971).

28. TLP 3.33.

29. PI §132, cf. §138.

30. Z §322.

31. L. Wittgenstein, *Schriften* 2 (Suhrkamp, Frankfurt, 1964), p. 52.

32. Wittgenstein, *Schriften* 2, §54.

33. R. Carnap, 'Theoretische Fragen und praktische Entscheidungen', *Natur und Geist*, 2 (1934), p. 259; repr. in H. Schleichert (ed.), *Logischer Empirismus — Der Wiener Kreis* (Wilhelm Fink, München, 1975), p. 175.

2

Was Wittgenstein a Neopositivist?

First of all, I think, it will be useful to clarify why I think this
question an interesting one and why an answer to it will help us
to get a better picture of the development of the Vienna Circle
than the usual one. It is quite obvious that to find an answer to
this seemingly queer question we have to know what it means to
be a neopositivist. I deliberately have chosen the term which is
used not only by the enemies of logical empiricism, but sometimes also by themselves, e.g. as the subtitle of the well-known
book by Victor Kraft on the origin and history of the Vienna
Circle.[1] So we will have to find a connotation for this name. I
shall not give a long list of necessary conditions which define a
'neopositivist', not to speak of sufficient ones. Nevertheless, it may
be helpful to keep in mind that the aims that are set out in the
first official statement comprise, firstly, the investigation of the
foundations of empirical and non-empirical sciences (the term
taken in its everyday sense); secondly, the clarification of philosophical questions; and, thirdly, the elimination all meaningless
propositions from science as well as from philosophy. The
method applied to achieve this goal was the logical analysis of the
linguistic and conceptual apparatus of science and philosophy. I
shall not analyse these aims further here. But a similar question
could arise concerning Wittgenstein. Those who think there are
two completely different philosophers, Wittgenstein I and Wittgenstein II, might want to hear which 'Wittgenstein' should be
the object of that question. What we are interested in should not
depend on any special interpretation of the kind of relation
between the early and the later philosophy of Wittgenstein, and
as this is not the place to criticise and correct the view of the two
Wittgensteins which I think is untenable,[2] I shall not go into this.

All of us are acquainted with the history of contemporary philosophy, which tells us that Wittgenstein gave birth to two philosophical schools or movements: between the two world wars to the Vienna Circle and after the second war to linguistic or Oxford philosophy. Indeed, it has quite often been said that the philosophy of the Circle 'is little more than a series of extended comments on fundamental work of Wittgenstein', namely, the *Tractatus logico-philosophicus*.[3] To evaluate this judgement we first of all have to give an outline of the rise of Logical Positivism in Vienna and then try to find out (or, to work out) if Wittgenstein's contribution to it made him something like a leader or conversely a hidden member of this group of philosophers. Since he never attended a session of the Circle, his influence could only be a mediate one, either through his written work or via verbal communications with some of the members. And we know that it was mainly Waismann who *within* the Circle was regarded as the appointed advocate of Wittgenstein's ideas, appointed by the editors of the book-series *Schriften zur wissenschaftlichen Weltauffassung*, Philipp Frank and Moritz Schlick. Already in 1928, when Carnap's *Outline of mathematical logic* (*Abriß der Logistik*) and Richard von Mises' book on *Probability* were published, the book by Waismann which should have given a systematic view and commentary on Wittgenstein's philosophy was announced as *Kritik der Philosophie durch die Logik*.[4] As Gordon P. Baker has pointed out: the papers by Waismann are the primary source for studying certain aspects of the history of the Vienna Circle, namely the relation of their work to Wittgenstein's.[5]

I do not want to deny the importance of Waismann's papers as a main source of how Wittgenstein *intended* to influence the work of the Circle. But Waismann's work can surely not serve as the main source of *understanding* the relation between the Circle and Wittgenstein. The project Waismann *initially* was to work out was to give a coherent and systematic account of the philosophy of the *Tractatus*. And, as we know from the published result, the much revised version of the German *Urtext* of this project, *The principles of linguistic philosophy*,[6] there are only a few chapters which are related to the *Tractatus* philosophy and these are critical examinations of those ideas which Wittgenstein himself criticised in his later period. So, only if we take Waismann's elucidations during the actual sessions of the Circle, his remarkable attempt to grasp the essence of Wittgenstein's new approaches, will we find an important indicator of the way Wittgenstein's changing ideas entered into the discussions of the group.

Just to give an example of the way the members of the Circle discussed Wittgenstein's ideas, I shall quote part of a debate about the 'Theses' in which Waismann gave a condensed compilation of a Tractarian thesis from the 1929 perspective of Wittgenstein.[7] In the minutes of the session of 3 June 1931, we find a discussion of the question of experiencing internal and external relations. Waismann was not present for this discussion. But, as you will notice, it was Schlick who more or less defended a position which otherwise could have been defended by Wittgenstein, namely, that we cannot experience *internal relations* but only external ones.

Schlick: We only can experience external relations not internal ones.

Hahn: Is the experience of 'lighter/-coloured/' [*heller*] between two colours an external or an internal relation?

Schlick: With external relations you could have an experience; between colours however subsist [*bestehen*] internal relations.

Neider: Then there does not exist an experience 'lighter-/coloured/' [*heller*]?

Schlick: 'Lighter/-coloured/' is an internal relation and, therefore, it cannot be experienced like the relation 'next to the right'.

Hahn: To the experience 'red' is coordinated a process in the retina and if I talk of 'lighter', there could be an appropriate chemical process in the brain coordinated to this; in this case there would not exist a difference between 'lighter' and 'red' and lighter would be an external relation.

Carnap: If I say, something is lighter than something else, I have a certain chemical process in the centre of perceiving in the brain. But this is trivial, since otherwise there could not occur a movement of the stoma [mouth]. This, therefore, is not enough, because then there would not exist any internal relations.

Hahn: Internal relations are the numbers.

Carnap: If I say 'smaller', concerning numbers, then I do have in my speech-centre also a certain process.

Hahn: The colour 'red' is coordinated to a process on the retina, but there does not in the same sense exist a coordination to a brain process in regard to the number '2'.

29

Schlick: It is important that that, what happens, does have a structural Gestalt [*Strukturgestalt*]. If there is an internal relation then it occurs as the Gestalt of the whole process [*Gesamtprozeß*]. If one does see a lighter or darker colour, then we have here a whole process [*Gesamtprozeß*], and 'lighter' is just a part and not given in the same way as the individual colours.

Carnap: The internal relation is not a particular process, but a certain determination, a property of the whole process [*Gesamtprozeß*].

Kaufmann: If I see two blue(s), one of this is lighter than the other, then this is an internal relation. If we speak of it, does 'lighter' not mean some isolating abstraction? It certainly is a relation, which does obtain also in regard to other classes of colour and what I can show here I can show there also; it is an invariant of the whole complex.

And somewhat later in the discussion Schlick remarks:

> If I speak of experiences of relations, I do mean that I had this experience aside from that other one. — Experiences of relations do not matter in regard to internal relations, since the latter ones are already given with them. They do not enter the proposition, but are shown in its form and unspeakable [*unaussprechbar*].

And he concludes this part of the discussion with the statement:

> It is wrong to ask, if one has an experience 'lighter' extra and apart from the other experiences.

First of all: we have here an original protocol of an actual session of the Circle. Sometimes these notes are quotations of what has been said by one member, most times they give a summary of the content of the discussions. The protocol had to be approved by the members and they could add to it. It would be of the utmost importance to publish them as soon as possible, at least in order to enforce the understanding of the varieties of views within the Circle.

Second: I think this is a typical example not only of how the members of the Circle went through every line of Waismann's thesis, but also of the way in which they accepted the Wittgensteinian approach and of how they criticised it. Even if the topics of the discussions were changed, the main points of perspectives to view them remained. And it is quite obvious that Waismann and very often Schlick were the advocates of Wittgenstein's point of view, while Neurath remained in strong opposition.

We may detect a similar line in Hahn's arguments. He did not want to accept that there are immediate given elements (like yellow, blue, the tone *a* etc.) — but defended the thesis that all those elements are already constructions out of the whole complex of instantaneous experience. Very often during their arguments he varies this point. So, for instance, in the session of 12 February 1931, when he underlines the statement that it would be wrong to assume that certain colour-signs force us to use a language of a certain determined structure. 'By facts we rule out only some language of a certain structure'. And when Schlick and Kaufmann reply that what is given forces upon us also a certain kind of sign-structure, or when they insist that language must have the same structure, or when they insist that language must have the same multiplicity as that which it denotes, then Hahn denies again that what is given in such a way should have a determined structure. '*Dies wäre Ontologie*' ('This would be ontology'). Carnap at this period mediated, so to speak, between the two sides. True, there was a strange tendency to overcome the differences and to reach a common and tenable view on the matters discussed, but if we look closer at the history of the Circle, we detect that the unity of tenets held by the members was soon again in danger of breaking off and it did break off in fact before the Circle was destroyed by external forces. Popper's bold conjecture that it was he who was responsible for the death of logical positivism can, however, not be taken seriously. The fact that there were strong philosophical tensions within the Circle was not completely unknown by the world at large. It became apparent particularly in the debate on protocol-sentences, that there were at least two groups of neo-empiricists to be distinguished: those who conceived of foundations of knowing and those who did not accept any such ultimate grounding on which the theories should be based. But, nevertheless, the tendency prevailed that the members of the Circle described themselves as a movement, which was bound to the tenets which were announced in the 1929 pamphlet: *Wissenschaftliche Weltauffassung: Der Wiener Kreis*. Only recently could I confirm the origin and actual authorship of this pamphlet. The first version was written by Neurath, but rejected by Carnap who then took over the task of giving it a balanced form. Feigl was also asked for co-operation at this stage. Thus when Carnap wrote to Schlick on 30 September 1929, presenting him with his copy of the *Wissenschaft-liche Weltauffassung*, he could say that it was compiled through a combined effort by Feigl, Neurath and himself.

> Den Inhalt betrachte bitte nicht zu kritisch, sondern mit Deinem gewohnten Wohlwollen und Nachsicht. Es ist von Feigl, Neurath und mir mit vereinten *Kräften* und mehr gutem Willen als Qualität geschaffen worden ... Die biblio-graphischen Angaben in der Broschüre hat jeder selbst gemacht; jedoch für Dich und Einstein Feigl, für Wittgen-stein Waismann, für Russell ich.

> Please do not consider the content too critically but with your usual kindness and indulgence. It has been composed by Feigl, Neurath and myself through a joint effort and with more good will than quality ... Each of us did our own bibliographical annotations; but those for you and Einstein were made by Feigl, the ones for Wittgenstein by Wais-mann, and the ones for Russell by myself.

I think that this passage, which is also confirmed by other letters, now solves once for all the difficult question of the authorship of the pamphlet.

I now turn back to the protocol of the discussion since I have chosen this piece for the purpose of explaining not only how they proceeded but also *what* was discussed at this stage. I think that the question of internal and external relations, also discussed in some articles by Aldo Gargani,[8] is an important one for an under-standing of Wittgenstein as well as for the Circle's interpretation of his work. Wittgenstein himself had a special interest in the notion of internal relations. He had already stated in the *Tracta-tus*: 'The structures of propositions stand to one another in inter-nal relations' (TLP 5.2). For instance, the internal relation which orders a series is equivalent to the operation by which one term is derived from another. Thus with the help of the notion of internal relation Wittgenstein wanted to elucidate the relation of proposi-tion to fact and with *this* the relation between language and real-ity. And he often propounds his idea in opposition to Russell (and in this case also to Ogden and Richards).[9] In the early thirt-ies, in the lecture notes taken by Lee and King, he explained the concept of internal relation as one 'given in the terms involved, in the nature of proposition and fact'. The character of these relations is — we are told — such that what they are relations of 'cannot be otherwise'.[10]

In order to attempt to clarify the notion of internal relations it will be useful to explain the internal–external distinction. To do this let us start from the intentional part of our language. If we intend something we are directed to what is intended in the same way as thought is to fact. How should this be understood? Well, the direction towards the object Wittgenstein calls the 'picture theory of meaning'. In the picture theory which Wittgenstein probably never gave up completely, even in his later period, only external relations can be expressed; internal relations however can only be shown. According to Russell (*The analysis of mind*) intentional states of the mind are like expectations. Against this Wittgenstein argues:

> for me, there are only two things involved in the fact that a thought is true, i.e. *the thought and the fact*; whereas for Russell there are three; thought, fact and a third event which, if it occurs, is just recognition. This third event, a sort of satisfaction of hunger, could for example be a feeling of pleasure.[11]

Since the intention however is determined by what is intended — that is by its internal relation, no further event, no external or causal relation is needed to describe it. If Russell were right, then if you have given an order to someone and you are satisfied with what he then does, this would amount to the fact that he has carried out the order.

I think that what can be said about this relation, which cannot be otherwise, is somehow similar to what can be said about the logical space within which something takes place: that what we expect and the expectation — both must be in the same space, or as we could also say, using some more familiar notion: they necessarily belong to *the same moves in a language game*. What you are describing then, in describing such a move, are *internal* relations, but not external ones.

I have added these remarks in order to explain what the discussion was about. But it is time to return to the main topic: Because I am not asking the question 'how did Wittgenstein's influence on the Vienna Circle work?' I want rather to find out if he himself may be labelled as a neopositivist — provided we do not provoke a debate about *names*. On the question of names, it is quite clear that members of the Circle did not like to be called positivists and that no one accepted the term 'neopositivist' as a proper name for the movement. Feigl, for instance, proposed the label '*logical* positivism' and Neurath quite often talked of a 'rational empiricism', a name he found in Itelson and not very different from the one used by Abel Rey: 'empirical rationalism'. Neurath liked the new, rediscovered *termini technici*: 'logical syntax', 'semantics', 'foundational research' (*Grundlagenforschung*) and the like, but he strongly disliked the term *positivism* no less than the term 'philosophy'. Writing to Carnap in April 1934 he stated:

> Daß Du das ekelhafte Wort exakte Philosophie, wissen-schaftliche Philosophie und so ähnlich überhaupt in den Mund und in die Feder nimmst, graust mir.

> That you take the horrible words 'exact philosophy', 'scien-tific philosophy' and similar ones into your mouth and that you write it also makes me sick.

Quite often Neurath mentions Comte's metaphysics as a real obstacle to using the term 'positivism' for the movement of the 'scientific world-conception'. For instance, he writes in a letter of 9 May 1934, commenting on the last version of Carnap's page-proofs of *Die Aufgaben der Wissenschaftslogik*:[12]

> Bitte nicht 'Positivismus' sagen. Ich las wieder mal Comtes Werk. Und obgleich ich es gegen zu viel Beschimpfung schützen muß, es graust einem oft ... Ich werde ihn bei 'Einheitswissenschaft' schon nennen — aber 'Positivismus' ... o weh.

> Please, don't say 'Positivism'. I once again have read the work of Comte. And in spite of the fact that I have to defend it against too much denunciation, it often does make one sick ... I shall surely mention him [namely Comte, R.H.] in regard to 'Unified Science — but 'positivism' ... oh woe!

Well, I do not want to add anything further. It is quite clear: no one of this group wanted to be a neopositivist or to be called one.

Those who were at all interested in the prehistory of their own approach did not deny the heritage from classical empiricism, but no one underlined a dominant relation to Comte or any other philosopher of that school.

At the beginning of this chapter I said it would be useful to know what the often-used term 'neopositivism' designates. If we look to those critics who have baptised a certain view of theory-construction as the *received view* and who have very often identified this view with the alleged theories of the Vienna Circle, we find a cliché which gets its force from simplifications. According to this picture, the neopositivists had *firstly* developed and defended a theory of knowledge derived from the faulty assumption that all statements or all meaningful statements are, in principle, derived from immediate experience (which should mean either that they can be translated into statements about immediate experiences, or that they are constituted out of elementary experiences); *secondly* it was held that the logical empiricists dismissed the diachrony of theories from their studies (that is, dismissed the historical perspective of science), and were solely interested in analytic and systematic problems of scientific theories; *thirdly* that the logical empiricists conceived the idea of cumulative progress in science. I think that all three of these suppositions are wrong and quite often in the last ten or fifteen years I have asked for a revision of our picture of the Vienna Circle. The supposed dogmas of the Circle were *not* tenets of the Circle and certainly not held during its heyday, and moreover they were already being criticised within the Circle. Indeed some members of the Circle never held them. Thus we find a short report to this effect in Carnap's diary for 22 February 1930: 'From 8 to 11 with Tarski in a Coffeehouse ... he thinks that there is only a gradual and subjective difference between tautological and empirical propositions.' And when Carnap converted to physicalism from his project of constructing a system based on structural properties and on the conviction that *every* scientific statement can be transformed into a statement which only contains structural properties and a description of the frame of objects, he was not quite clear how the language which states the immediate experiences was to be analysed. There was more confusion than unanimity about the concept of immediate experiences. As a result, in correspondence he accuses Neurath of creating confusion by starting a discussion on the nature of proto-col-sentences, when it was still not clear *what the right analysis should be.*[13]

35

But what was even stranger was that as soon as Wittgenstein received Carnap's article 'Die physikalische Sprache als Universalsprache der Wissenschaften' ('The physicalistic language as universal language of science') (*Die physikalische Sprache als Universalsprache der Wissenschaften*),[14] he accused Carnap of plagiarism, especially concerning the idea of *physicalism*. He said to Carnap in a letter of 30 August 1932 that, since Carnap had not mentioned *his* name, he had misled the readers about the main source (*'die Hauptquelle'*) of his ideas. And in a letter to Schlick of 8 August of the same year (written also in Hochreit) he says: 'Daß ich mich nicht mit der Frage des "Physikalismus" befaßt hätte, ist unwahr (nur nicht unter diesem — scheußlichen — Namen und in der Kürze, in der die ganze "Abhandlung" geschrieben ist.'[15] And he goes on to tell Schlick that Carnap has also taken his view of *hypotheses* and he even thinks that the distinction of formal and material mode of speaking is no step beyond his own point of view.

Here we see Wittgenstein claiming the provenance of those ideas which in the usual histories of the development of the neopositivistic movement are already seen as important steps beyond the original sensationalistic basis. He claims that this interpretation can be found in the *Tractatus*, which was finished in 1918. However we may take sides in these accusations, I think they encourage a reconsideration of the real history of the Circle. Neurath, whom Carnap also claimed should be considered as the main source of physicalism, suggested that it would be less misleading to talk of a 'Vienna Circle of *Physicalism*' than of the scientific 'world outlook', since the term 'world outlook' (*Weltauffassung*) is often mistaken for *Weltanschauung*.[16]

Perhaps it is time now to put our discussion on Wittgenstein's position within the Circle into a wider frame. Therefore, I suggest looking at the Vienna Circle in the following way: first of all, there were two Vienna Circles. The first came into existence around 1907 and lasted until about 1912. Its principal members were Hans Hahn, Philipp Frank, and Otto Neurath. The main topics of *their* Thursday discussions were the problems of the philosophy of science, methodology, but, as we know from Frank, also political, historical, and even religious problems were discussed. The group was very much under the influence of Mach. And it was mainly the difficulties which derived from a comparison of some of the results of Poincaré, Duhem, and Abel Rey which they could not easily solve. We have to take into account that the works of the French conventionalists had been

translated into German almost immediately after their publication in France. The translation of *La théorie physique: son objet et sa
structure* came out only two years after the French edition with a
preface by E. Mach. And in the same year the Viennese Rudolf
Eisler edited a German translation of Abel Rey's *Theory of physics*.
If you consider that the first translation of Duhem into English
was published almost fifty years later — namely 1954 — it is easy
to imagine why the conventionalistic and especially the holistic
view of laws and scientific tendencies entered the positivistic
discussion so early. The idea that however a hypothesis may
enter into a theory it may be sustained in the face of a recalitrant
experience and the thesis that every datum may be described in
many different ways by a theoretical symbolism[17] lead to the view
that all empirical propositions, even the *Protokollsätze*, which we
use in confirmation procedures, are chosen on the basis of *deci-
sions* and can, in principle, be changed and revised. By 1913
Neurath had, for instance, developed a dynamic and diachronic
view of changing theories on this basis, asking for a theoretical
understanding of theory-change. Perhaps one of the most interesting results of the cooperation within the first Vienna Circle at
the end of the first decade of this century was the formulation of
what I have dubbed the 'Neurath-principle'. This principle is
certainly derived from Duhem and says: if we accept a holistic
view of theories, then we are always in the happy position of
having two options concerning a proposition which is not coherent with the whole system: *either* change the proposition which
you would like to cohere with the system *or* change the system.
According to Occam's razor you have to accomplish this change
in the most economical way in order to simplify the system and
the understanding of the facts in question. Much later, in 1935,
Neurath — who had not changed his conception of theories at all
— wrote that we cannot deny that the actual encyclopedias (that
is the notion he then preferred to that of 'system' or 'theory') can
be compared with model encyclopedias, which are freed from the
faults of contradictions. But even in regard to them, we could
never seriously state and judge an isolated statement. Validity
can only be affirmed in connection with the mass of existing and
so far accepted statements. And with respect to this, every proposition is open to revision.[18] Similar ideas have been proposed by
Frank and also held by Hahn.

Well, I do not have time here to expose the ideas of the first
Vienna Circle even in general, not to speak of the details. But if

we want to understand the history of the better-known movement of the twenties and early thirties, we have to take into account the existence of the *first Circle*. It was because of this that Philipp Frank could truly say in Hahn's obituary in 1934, that the *real founder* of the Vienna Circle was Hahn.

Actually it was he who could convince the faculty to put Schlick on the list and it was he who convinced the members of the mathematical seminar — Radakovic, Waismann, Gödel, Menger, and Bergmann — to attend Schlick's Thursday meetings as Schlick was, after all, the only full professor of Philosophy in the Circle. And it was again Hahn who, after the study of Frege and Russell, asked for an interpretation of the *Logisch-philoso-phische Abhandlung*.

At this point we return to Wittgenstein: and since here I can rely on a large body of knowledge of historical facts in the remainder of this paper I can try to explain why our question, whether Wittgenstein was a neopositivist, cannot have a yes or no answer.

And the reasons for this uncertainty are — as I said in the beginning — to be found in the vagueness of the connotations of the two names: neopositivist and Wittgenstein. I do not know which is the more difficult to resolve. Because if we agree that there was a first Vienna Circle formed by a proper part of that well-known group of logical empiricists, called by Neurath *Der Wiener Kreis*, we have to acknowledge that there have been very different views on almost all important questions through all the periods of its existence: not only different views, but also views which *contradicted one another*. Contrary to the standard interpretations we have to consider the influence of Wittgenstein not as starting a school-movement, not as dominating from the beginning, but rather like the passage of a comet against a backdrop of stars. For a short period some members of the group of philosophers, mathematicians and sociologists around Schlick were fascinated by the light of this comet. But as we know — not all of them.

It is not appropriate at this point to map the influence and to point out *why* the members of the first Vienna Circle, Hahn, Frank, and Neurath, never felt tempted to change their own view of philosophy of science for the one held by Wittgenstein. Their view was a naturalistic conception of science *and* philosophy which accepted the pragmatic and conventionalist of Poincaré and Duhem on the one hand, and Mach, Einstein, and Russell on the other. I must concede that in a superficial interpretation of some of the writings of Frank and Hahn it may look as if they followed the usual phenomenalistic reading of Mach. But this interpretation itself derives from an untenable interpretation of Mach's complicated theory of elements because Mach held that we have to conceive of elements as the objects of *either* a phenomenological (psychological) *or* a physicalist interpretation of events. Therefore, when Philipp Frank summarised the main achievements of Mach's philosophy in an article published in 1917, he first pointed to the idea of the *unity of science* conceived by Mach in order to provide a consistent link between physics on the one hand, and physiology and psychology on the other. Secondly, however, he praised Mach for being the philosopher who preserved the heritage of the Enlightenment for our time. And the means to achieve this was the principle of economy which made it possible to criticise seemingly meaningful utterances postulating entities which do not exist. An utterance or a proposition, according to Mach, is senseless if it contains signs which are pseudo-descriptive; which means, signs for which we cannot find an empirical interpretation for their meaning.

It was not difficult for members of the first Vienna Circle to read the relevant passages of the *Tractatus* as a clarifying interpretation of these two Machian principles. Wherever in the discussions of Waismann's thesis they suspected a different understanding of the two principles we find them *in opposition* to Wittgenstein. This applies to Frank, Hahn, and Neurath. From the early days — as we know — Neurath was the strongest opponent of Wittgenstein's conception of the unspeakable as the most important part of his philosophy.

So, when I say that the Viennese philosophers accepted Wittgenstein's conception of philosophy stated in the dictum 'All philosophy is critique of language' (TLP 4.003) ('Alle Philosophie ist Sprachkritik'), I do not mean that Neurath approved of the Wittgensteinian approach as such. But he certainly accepted the idea that only science can produce true pictures, models of reality, and he was in complete accordance with Wittgenstein when he stated that only what can clearly be asked at all will also be clearly answered; it makes no sense to talk of unsolvable riddles.[19] But Neurath never gave an exact analysis of the conditions of clarity. When he used the notion of clarity he did not consider internal relations at all. He was only interested in the consensus of scientists as to the acceptance of propositions of any given kind.

The scheme he proposed to test the sense of a proposition is the same as the scheme for deciding the truth-value of the proposition: namely, the confrontation with the whole system of propositions accepted within a certain community so far. This was the route he had learned to follow from Poincaré to Duhem, and as we know, he never gave up following it. Only one of his consequences was that there could not be a test of any singular hypothesis. Or as Carnap put it in 1934 — mentioning the names of Poincaré and Duhem in parentheses: 'The test applies ... not to a single hypothesis but to the whole system of physics as a system of hypotheses.'[20]

We know how Schlick replied to this idea, which was completely alien to him: 'If anyone should tell me that I believe in the truth of science ultimately because it has been adopted by "the scientists of my cultural Circle" I should ... smile at him',[21] and he points to the fact that in some way or other everybody has to test the truthworthiness of the beliefs held by the (other) scientists. It is quite clear that the proposal of the testing-scheme cannot be used to clarify the meanings of the propositions to be tested. They are said to be hypotheses which get their meaning via verification and their truth either by their coherence with other propositions or not at all.

It seems to me that *behind* the heavy misunderstandings concerning the problem of sense as well as the problem of verification and testing lies a confusion of psychological and semantic questions, or perhaps more clearly of epistemic and non-epistemic uses of the key notions in the description of science as a system and as an activity. It is a confusion similar to that between linguistic rules and rules of behaviour, provided we understand the former in the sense of a grammar as Wittgenstein did. I think that Wittgenstein himself tried to avoid the confusion when he started to criticise his own conception of the elementary propositions as well as the *Tractatus* theory of names. But I am not convinced that he succeeded.

Like Schlick, Carnap, Neurath, and most of the members of the Vienna School, he believed that metaphysical questions are ruled out by a meaning-criterion: by stating the conditions which make a statement true. And he also believed — like the others — that the verification of a statement is the procedure which does in fact fulfil this task.

When he proceeds in his research on the 'grammar of language', he very often remarks that his questions are psychological and he confronts them using external criteria. In a manuscript of 1931, not yet published, he asks 'What has what I think, to do with what is the case?'[22] And again he doubts:

> The question namely is this: is all, that I am doing here not mythology? Do I not add poetically to what is already apparent, when I speak of the process which is going on in understanding (meaningfully uttering or hearing) the sentence?
>
> That is, couldn't I consider language as a social institution, subordinated to certain rules, because otherwise it would not be effective. But then: That latter is something I cannot say: even so I cannot give a justification of the rule. I could describe it only as a game which human beings undertake.[23]

He developed the idea of *Sprachspiele* and he notes, exaggerating as he often does, that there are uncountably many of them. And in the *Remarks on the philosophy of psychology* we find in double brackets a hint as to what alternatives he had in mind when he proposed his new ideas: '((There are more language games than Carnap and others have dared to dream.))'[24]

I am coming to the end of my paper which should have given an answer to the question: was Wittgenstein a neopositivist? I have tried to provide some arguments for the assumption that almost no member of the two Circles accepted being called a positivist and I have provided some reasons for the correction of the received view of logical positivism.[25]

When Wittgenstein read the 1929 pamphlet: *Wissenschaftliche Weltauffassung*, he reminded Waismann that the important task is not the propaganda or *Großsprecherei* but the philosophical activity, that is, what is *done* by the Vienna Circle.

I think in this he was completely right: it is not the thesis that counts in philosophy. What the Viennese School is able to do, Wittgenstein thought, has to be *shown* not to be *said*: '*Das Werk muß den Meister loben.*' ('The work should praise the master.')

And I think that the philosophical work done by the neopositivists who did not want to be called so does indeed praise its masters: it remains the standard we use to evaluate the philosophical work of our time.

Notes

1. V. Kraft: *Der Wiener Kreis. Der Ursprung des Neopositivismus. Ein Kapitel der jüngsten Philosophiegeschichte*, 2nd enlarged edn (Springer, Wien, 1968). Cf. A.J. Ayer (ed.), *Logical positivism* (Free Press, Glencoe, Ill., 1959).

2. R. Haller, 'Ludwig Wittgenstein und die Österreichische Philosophie', *Wissenschaft und Weltbild*, 21 (1968), reprinted in R. Haller, *Studien zur Österreichischen Philosophie* (Rodopi, Amsterdam, 1979), p. 120.

3. *Vide* J.R. Weinberg, *An examination of logical positivism* (Routledge & Kegan Paul, London 1936), p. 26.

4. *Vide* R. von Mises, *Wahrscheinlichkeit Statistik und Wahrheit* (Schriften zur wissenschaftlichen Weltauffassung, 3) (J. Springer, Wien, 1928).

5. G.P. Baker, 'Verehrung und Verkehrung: Waismann and Wittgenstein', in C.G. Luckhardt (ed.), *Wittgenstein, sources and perspectives* (Harvester, Hassocks, 1979), p. 280.

6. F. Waismann, *The principles of linguistic philosophy*, ed. R. Harré (Macmillan, London, 1965). Cf. F. Waismann, *Logik, Sprache und Philosophie*, Preface by Moritz Schlick, ed. G.P. Baker & B.F. McGuinness together with J. Schulte (Reclam, Stuttgart, 1976).

7. The 'Theses' are published in the *Schriften* by Ludwig Wittgenstein and their actual discussion within the Circle took place in 1931.

8. A. Gargani, 'Schlick and Wittgenstein: language and experience' in R. Haller (ed.), *Schlick und Neurath — Ein Symposion* (Rodopi, Amsterdam, 1982), pp. 347-63, reprinted in S.G. Shanker (ed.), *Ludwig Wittgenstein: critical assessments* (Croom Helm, London, 1984), vol. 1, pp. 275-86.

9. B. Russell, *The analysis of mind* (Allen and Unwin, London, 1921), p. 75f.

10. Desmond Lee (ed.), *Wittgenstein's Lectures, Cambridge 1930-32* (Roman & Littlefield, Tatowa, N.J., 1980), pp. 9f.

11. L. Wittgenstein, *Philosophical remarks*, III, §21.

12. R. Carnap, *Die Aufgaben der Wissenschaftslogik* (Einheitswissenschaft, Schriften, vol. 3, ed. O. Neurath together with R. Carnap and H. Hahn (Vienna, 1934).

13. Unpublished letter from Carnap to Neurath; cf. J. Vuillemin, 'Physicalism and relativity', in R. Haller (ed.), *Schlick und Neurath — Ein Symposion* (Rodopi, Amsterdam, 1982), pp. 314ff.

14. R. Carnap, 'Die physikalische Sprache als Universalsprache der Wissenschaft', *Erkenntnis*, 2 (1931).

15. 'It is untrue that I had not concerned myself with the question of "physicalism" (only not under this hideous title, and only in that brevity in which the whole [*Tractatus*] is written).'

16. O. Neurath, 'Soziologie im Physikalismus', *Erkenntnis*, 2 (1931), reprinted in Otto Neurath, *Gesammelte philosophische und methodologische Schriften*, ed. R. Haller and H. Rutte (2 vols, Hölder-Pichler-Tempsky, Vienna, 1981), vol. 2, pp. 533-62. English translation by M. Magnus and R. Raico as 'Sociology and physicalism' in Ayer (ed.), *Logical positivism*, pp. 282-371. Cf. Ayer (ed.), *Logical positivism*, p. 282.

17. Cf. J. Vuillemin, 'On Duhem's and Quine's theses', *Grazer Philosophische Studien*, 9 (1979), pp. 69-96. *Vide* also R. Haller, 'Der erste Wiener

Kreis' in W.K. Essler (ed.) *Epistemology, methodology, and philosophy of science. Essays in honour of Carl G. Hempel on the occasion of his 80th birthday (January 8th, 1985)* (Reidel, Dordrecht-Boston, 1985: *Erkenntnis*, 22 (1985)), pp. 341-59.

18. R. Haller, 'Über Otto Neurath', in his *Studien zur Österreichischen Philosophie* (Rodopi, Amsterdam, 1979), vol. 1, ch. VII, pp. 95-105; Haller, 'Der erste Wiener Kreis'; R. Haller, 'Das Neurath-Prinzip — Grundlagen und Folgerungen', in F. Stadler (ed.) *Arbeiterbildung in der Zwischenkriegszeit. Otto Neurath — Gerd Arntz* (Löcker, Vienna, 1982). O. Neurath, 'Physicalism and the investigation of knowledge' in Otto Neurath, *Philosophical papers 1913-1946*, ed. R.S. Cohen and M. Neurath (Reidel, Dordrecht, 1983), p. 161. *Vide* H. Rutte, 'Der Philosoph Otto Neurath' in Stadler (ed.), *Arbeiterbildung in der Zwischenkriegszeit*, pp. 70-8.

19. O. Neurath, 'Wege der wissenschaftlichen Weltauffassung' in Neurath, *Gesammelte philosophische und methodologische Schriften*, ed. R. Haller and H. Rutte.

20. R. Carnap, *The logical syntax of language* (London, 1937), p. 318.

21. M. Schlick, 'Facts and propositions', *Analysis*, 2 (1935), p. 69; repr. in M. Schlick, *Collected papers*, vol. II (1925-36), ed. H. Mulder & B.B.F. van der Velde-Schlick (Reidel, Dordrecht-Boston-London, 1979), pp. 400-4. Compare the excellent paper by A. Coffa, 'Carnaps Sprachauffassung circa 1932', *PSA*, 1976, p. 219.

22. L. Wittgenstein, Manuscript, p. 135: 'Was hat das, was ich denke, mit dem zu tun, was der Fall ist?'

23. L. Wittgenstein, Manuscript, p. 195: 'Die Frage ist aber nämlich: ist alles, was ich hier treibe, nicht Mythologie? Dichte ich nicht zu dem offenbaren dazu /hinzu/; wenn ich nämlich von dem Vorgang rede, der beim Verstehen (verständnisvollen Aussprechen oder Hören) des Satzes vor sich geht.

D.h. könnte ich nicht die Sprache als soziale Einrichtung betrachten, die gewissen Regeln unterliegt, weil sie sonst nicht wirksam wäre /wirksam würde/. Aber hier liegt es: dies letztere /letzte/ kann ich nicht sagen: eine Rechtfertigung der Regel kann ich, auch so, nicht geben. Ich könnte sie nur als ein Spiel, das die Menschen betreiben, beschreiben.'

24. L. Wittgenstein, *Remarks on the philosophy of psychology*, I, §920: '((Es gibt eben viel mehr Sprachspiele, als Carnap und Andere sich träumen lassen.))'.

25. Cf. R. Haller, 'New Light on the Vienna Circle', *Monist*, 65 (1982), pp. 25-37.

3

Was Wittgenstein a Neo-Kantian?

One of the demands of the orderly mind is that novel objects or occurrences in history be ordered under an interpretative schema already familiar to us. However complex and many-faceted a work of literature might be, our pursuit of understanding is often an attempt to frame it within *one* interpretation in order to make comprehensible, in terms of the framework, the relationship between the facets and layers of the work, and the unified whole.

Common interpretative schemata are also frequently characteristic of philosophical schools which adopt the basic principles of some doctrine, whether that doctrine is a traditional one or of recent origin. These basic principles can just as well be of a methodological as of a substantive nature. In the first instance, they concern the manner of knowing and the means of acquiring knowledge, and they result in the exclusion of other procedures, for which rationalism and empiricism provide examples; in the second case, they govern the description of existent beings, between the extremes of idealism and realism (just to mention two of our more crude classificatory schemata).

As I have already pointed out, philosophical schools of thought frequently originate with the disciples of an influential teacher or scholar, whose merit inheres in having reflected upon such perspectives in novel ways, having put innovative questions and traced new routes to the solution of old ones. Occasionally however, philosophical schools originate when a traditional doctrine is *revived* because of an interest in hitherto undiscovered or undiscussed aspects, and the essential principles of the original doctrine are brought to bear upon historically altered situations and a changed state of the art.

I believe that the existence of historicising accounts has particular significance for the philosophical attempt to create unified systems, in that it appears to undermine the general claim that every genuinely philosophical thought more or less implies, namely that of having expressed a truth which — as Wittgenstein said — is 'incontestable and definitive'.

We must, therefore, distinguish between the fact of historical contingency given by the sociocultural dimension of a historically determined situation, and historical relativity, which implies the contingency of validity claims by placing all phenomena within the framework of a historical narrative. A historically conditioned discovery, like Copernicus' discovery of the movements of the planets, can be true, just as the assertion of historical determinacy and relativity can be false and may turn out to be a mere emanation of a certain sociocultural situation.

If the question is raised as to whether Wittgenstein was a neo-Kantian, then regardless of how the question is answered, the answer should be motivated neither by reductive intentions nor by a sceptical intent to relativise the significance of his work. Clearly it is not obvious why one should integrate the founder of one school of thought — and Wittgenstein was regarded as such among small circles in the 30s — to some other school of thought. Let us ask, then, what arguments can be brought in support of representing Wittgenstein as a neo-Kantian, and secondly, what reasons there are for regarding such an epithet as a false one. Before considering these questions in detail, the conditions under which we would be disposed to answer the original question in the affirmative or in the negative should be specified. Furthermore I shall proceed in such a way as to show why the question is one that needs to be considered at all, and I shall then turn to the historical questions.

A number of Wittgenstein's 'exegetes' were early persuaded that Wittgenstein's philosophy ought not to be regarded merely against the backdrop of Frege's and Russell's influence in England, but rather ought to be viewed from the vantage point of the wider currents in continental philosophy. Interestingly, they began not with an interpretation of the *Tractatus*, but, in the first instance, with an interpretation of the *Philosophical investigations*. As early as 1962, Stanley Cavell[1] drew a parallel between the concept of a 'grammatical' investigation in Wittgenstein's sense, and that of a transcendental investigation. But precisely what was the claim being made here, and what were the arguments brought in its support?

According to Cavell, Wittgenstein *himself* had indicated that the manner in which he conducted his investigations might be called *transcendental*. This would have been a striking remark indeed, and a signal to the reader that could not be neglected without detriment to the interpretation. However, a closer look at the evidence shows us that the text does not support this judgement. In its favour the ninetieth of the 693 numbered paragraphs in the first part of the *Philosophical investigations* springs to mind. Here the locution, so typical of transcendental writing, seems to stand out on the page: '... our investigation, however, is directed not towards phenomena, but, as one might say, towards the "possibilities" of phenomena'. Of course, it not only *appears* that Kant is speaking here; he actually is, for the expression 'possibility' is introduced by Wittgenstein in quotation marks. Any philosopher is familiar with the position in consequence of which Kant called all cognition transcendental 'which is occupied not so much with objects as with the mode of our knowledge of objects in so far as this mode of knowledge is to be possible *a priori*'. (*Critique of pure reason*, 'Introduction' VII (A 12)). And in the Appendix to the *Prolegomena to any future metaphysics*, a footnote states that the transcendental does not signify something 'passing beyond all experience but something that indeed precedes it *a priori*, but that is intended simply to make knowledge of experience possible'.[2]

Still, Wittgenstein does elucidate the expression 'possibility of phenomena' by equating its sense with the '*kind of statement* that we make about phenomena'. But the example that he introduces already serves to warn us that it would be absurd to attempt to discover parallels between Kant and Wittgenstein in this passage. After indicating that it is the *kind* of statement that is to be of interest, Wittgenstein's ensuing remark in this passage, which begins with Augustine's question 'Quid est ergo tempus?', states: 'Thus Augustine recalls to mind the different statements that are made about the duration, past, present, or future, of events.' Wittgenstein subsequently terms such an investigation 'grammatical'. It might appear that this is only one step — at least for Stanley Cavell and also, perhaps, for Peter Hacker — from substituting the concept of the transcendental for that of grammar. The kinds of things that can be said seem most likely to correspond to the categories, which in Kantian usage are the pure concepts of the understanding. There are, for Kant, just as many pure concepts of the understanding concerned with the objects of perception as there are logical functions in judgements and, indeed, in all possible judgements. Building upon these assumptions, Kant can derive the concept of synthesis from the table of judgements, viz. the possibilities, or even capacity, of thought. We find nothing of the kind in Wittgenstein. We find nothing of this kind in Wittgenstein, against whom Kant could have made the same reproach as he made against Aristotle, namely, having selected these concepts just by chance (*'aufs bloße Urgefähr'*). For in Wittgenstein's entire opus, there is not one attempt to set out a table of categories. One could counter that it is part of the very uniqueness of Wittgenstein's *Philosophical investigations*, that in place of a determinate *a priori* order of things, the manifold of *actual* kinds of statements is taken as the basis of analysis. If this were done, the rather restrictive Kantian table of judgements would be considerably widened, though the procedure itself would not be so very distinguishable from the Kantian procedure. But even an author like Peter Hacker, who alleges that he has discovered similarities between Wittgenstein and the Königsberg scholar at every possible (and impossible) point, concedes: 'The spirit of Kant's transcendental dialectic and doctrine of method was totally foreign to Wittgenstein.'[4] Hacker obviously means, here, to refer to limitations in the systematic development of the programme of the *Critique*, rather than to a fundamental difference between Kant and Wittgenstein. However, as I hope to show, this judgement too is erroneous.

It is necessary first of all to attain some clarity about what is to be understood by the expression 'grammatical investigation'. A grammatical investigation is, in Wittgenstein's linguistic phenomenology, an investigation of the nature of an object. ('Grammar tells what kind of object anything is' PI I §373.) Indeed, *'Essence* is expressed by grammar' (PI I §371). If one knows what 'grammar' means, then one also knows what is to be understood by 'essence'. It is certainly not a *hypokeimenon*, an *ousia* in Aristotle's sense, something that would enter a definition. But what something — e.g. an object — *is* cannot be derived from what it is not. Already in the *Philosophical grammar* from the early 30s,[5] Wittgenstein writes: 'It does not belong to grammar, that this observation sentence is true and that one false. To it belong all conditions (the methods) of the comparison of the sentence with reality. That is, all conditions of the understanding (of sense).'[6] These remarks about the conditions that belong to grammar make it apparent that Wittgenstein understood the grammatical investigation in much more comprehensive terms than could be covered by logical syntax. If, in fact, grammar already contains *all* forms of representation, then grammar could also determine, *a priori*, what essence belongs necessarily to an object.

It appears that no empirical investigation could reveal the essence of such things as a mental image, an inner experience, a wish, or the like, while the conditions of understanding, like those of meaning, hold fast. Thus philosophy, the 'custodian of grammar', gives no explanations, but only descriptions. If philosophy were to take it upon itself to analyse events in world history, empirical phenomena in the common sense of the term, then every case would have to be shown to be an instance of a law conforming to the category of causality. But the *connection* between the use of an expression and the conditions or rules of its employment, or of the comparison of a sentence with reality, is never shown in experience, although it is by the grace of nature that we do possess knowledge. That is to say, our forming a new judgement naturally presupposes that the expressions which describe a fact correspond to the rules of grammar. That we recognise its truth, know *that it is so*, presupposes that nature behaves as we say it does. But if it is true that grammar includes the rules that we have extracted from it, this is still no proof that a given rule is itself necessary, and universally valid. Necessity and universal validity are, however — according to Kant — the criteria of the *a priori*. Now there can be no doubt that Wittgenstein was intent on showing that the criteria of grammaticality are *not* universal validity and necessity. Therefore, while we need not give up the image of language as a calculus, that image must be recast. In fact, one could say that grammar is a calculus. But grammar doesn't say that it itself *is also* the employment of the calculus. This sounds cryptic, and it is. But one would not want to maintain that Wittgenstein was successful in developing this principal theme of his philosophy to the point that he had intended, namely to the point of clarity and perspicuity. However, it would also be rash to maintain that the interpreters had somehow recovered what Wittgenstein overlooked.[7]

Neither is now the time to recover what might have been overlooked. For our purposes, it must suffice to point out those factors which show themselves to be of *relative* importance and consequence. Accordingly, a grammatical investigation can be understood, first, as an investigation into the use of the words in a language. 'Grammar describes the use of words in a language. So it has somewhat the same relation to language as the description of a game, the rules of a game, have to the game' (PG I 23). Secondly, it follows that a grammatical investigation includes a description of the rules of a language game. Those sentences which reproduce or describe rules do not describe behaviour, states of affairs, or events. Such sentences describe conceptual connections and have, for this reason, no empirical character. What lends to these sentences a status that misleads one into thinking of them as synthetic *a priori* is not a capacity to extend our knowledge, nor is it that they are universally valid, but rather a peculiar combination of empirical content and necessity inherent in them. The reason for this is to be found in the fact that the rules are concerned with use, and thus have a semantic component which is empirical, while as rules they cannot be true or false. Their necessary, although logically arbitrary, connection with use, which determines their meaning, lends autonomy to them and to language. 'The rules of grammar may be called 'arbitrary', if that is to mean that the *aim* of the grammar is nothing but that of the language' (PI I §497).[8]

Yet already very early, in his conversations with Waismann, Wittgenstein states:

> In grammar you cannot discover anything. There are no surprises. When formulating a rule we always have the feeling: That is something you have known all along. We can do only one thing — clearly articulate the rule we have been applying unawares. If, then, I understand what the specification of a length means, I also know that, if a man is 1.6 m tall, he is not 2 m tall. I know that a measurement determines only *one* value on a scale and not several values. If you ask me, How do I know that? I shall simply answer, Because I understand the sense of the statement. It is impossible to understand the sense of such a statement without knowing the rule ... Thus if I understand the sense of a proposition at all, I must also understand the syntax of an expression occurring in it. You cannot discover anything in grammar, you can only elucidate.[9]

It becomes clear that the sentences that belong to the grammar of a language cannot be synthetic sentences, which also shows that they are to be distinguished from all law-like propositions. In this passage — as in numerous others — we learn that there is a close connection between understanding an expression and what might be called the grammaticality of an expression. It is exceedingly difficult to name the presuppositions and preconditions of grammaticality. But it is relatively simple to state what Wittgenstein counts among the conditions of grammaticality, the content of the grammar book: namely, agreement among judgements and ultimately, agreement in action.[10] That is to say, if we were not to agree in the naming of colours, and in our use of colour words, then the question of *whether* an object is or is not of a certain colour could not meaningfully be asked — or if asked, could not be meaningfully answered. If one cannot presume agreement among the systems and scales of measurement, then there are no values to determine. I have argued elsewhere that these agreements are not mere conventions attaching to certain purposes, but rather the expression of a praxeological foundationalism, for which it holds that communicative action is itself a condition of the agreement among actions as among judgements.[11]

My purpose here is to show that the grammatical investigation is not, in Wittgenstein's judgement, a transcendental one. Before turning again to this task, however, I would like to consider a third sense of the term 'grammatical investigation'. This third sense concerns what Wittgenstein refers to in several passages as the 'grammatical sentence'. Grammatical sentences are distinguished from empirical sentences firstly in that they function as presuppositions for empirical sentences, and secondly, in that they have the character of definitions or explications of concepts, but, in contrast to empirical sentences, do not represent a move in a language game, and stand in no causal relation to the world.

Sentences like 'Every rod has a length', 'White is lighter than black' (RFM I, §104), 'The class of lions is not a lion', 'This body has extension' (PI I §252), 'Green and blue can't be in the same place simultaneously' (BB p. 56) state that we could not have named something a 'rod' if it had no length, that something could not be white, without being brighter than something black, and that something is not a body which is not extended. If we nonetheless use these negative formulations, then we are changing their meanings; giving them new ones. To say: 'The measuring rod *has* a length' is, in a sense, just as absurd as saying 'The measuring rod has no length', although we would tend to regard empirical satisfaction as confirmation of the meaningfulness of the sentence. However, it is a mistake (a 'confusion'), according to Wittgenstein, to consider grammatical sentences as capable of verification or falsification. Only empirical sentences can be verified or falsified.

> When we hear both the sentence 'This rod has a length' and its negation 'This rod has no length', we are partial and incline towards the first sentence; instead of declaring both to be nonsense.[12]

Although this third way of speaking of grammatical investigations, which has led us to the grammatical sentence, appears to be analogous to the analytic investigation, which results in analytic sentences — sentences which are true in virtue of the meanings of the expressions in them — nowhere does Wittgenstein use this characterisation, which is originally a Kantian one.

Thus, the concept of an *a priori* truth — necessary for the determination of synthetic *a priori* judgements — also leads to absurd consequences. But how is a transcendental question to be possible, if it is not concerned with synthetic *a priori* judgements? From what we have seen, Wittgenstein apparently didn't even regard putative analytic sentences as meaningful, that is, true or false, sentences, but rather attributed to them some other status. The reason for this is that Wittgenstein was convinced that if a sentence is meaningful, then its negation must also be meaningful, and vice versa.

Thus we see that the grammatical investigation, in which some have attempted to find parallels with the transcendental, in fact provides a convincing parallel in none of the three principal readings offered here, because the basis upon which the question arises is not sufficiently homogeneous, and the aim of the *Philosophical investigations* differs fundamentally from that of a transcendental investigation.

One could respond by asking whether the kinship or similarity claimed to exist between Wittgenstein and Kant doesn't exist in some other, and perhaps more substantial, respect.[13] Is it not perhaps correct, one could ask, that there is already in the *Tractatus* a 'Kantian tone' which justifies the characterisation of the work as a 'piece of critical philosophy',[14] and, moreover, is it not correct that this tone — relieved of its rationalist and ahistorical tendencies — is preserved in the later writings up to the notes *On certainty*? Isn't it possible that Wittgenstein was of the persuasion that mind *forms* nature? These are many questions in one, and I would rather not take it upon myself to pursue them all, or attempt solid answers. For Hacker, it appears that there is no need to doubt that there will be positive answers to all of these questions, since in his book, he just presupposes them. That is what I would call modelling nature (that is, here, Wittgenstein's writings) according to mind (here, the interpreter).

I believe that there is a superficial but wide-spread error in expecting results from a comparison of the Wittgensteinian conception of philosophy as critique of language, which he never abandoned, with the Kantian notion of a critique of reason and the Kantian aim of deriving an autonomous responsibility from rationality. 'Critique of language' is, however, the term used by Wittgenstein to denote the essential character of philosophy in the *Tractatus.* Indeed in a general sense: 'All philosophy is critique of language.' That Kant did *not* intend his critical philosophy primarily as an investigation into language was, already for Hamann and Herder, the point of strongest criticism. Hamann and Herder are also the authors that Mauthner, among several others, places in the family tree of those to whom the critique of language is, as Hamann put it, the Alpha and Omega of philosophy.[15] One cannot simply call every non-dogmatic, non-sceptical attempt at grounding experience a 'critical' one in the Kantian sense, because this would render the specifically Kantian point of departure quite empty. Wittgenstein's understanding of what counts as 'critique of language' is not derived from an understanding of the critique of reason, nor does it share its aim, even though, naturally, all critiques of metaphysics agree in their object of study. The *Critique of pure reason* is not only a critique of metaphysics, but rather a treatise on method and a justification of the conditions of mathematics and physics as the basic disciplines of natural science, in so far as this is to be done in conformity with natural law. The aim of Kantian philosopy is not the suspension of reason in the area of 'problems of life', but rather the suspension of immature thinking (the immaturity of which one oneself is to blame).[16] Taken in such a broad sense, the 'Regulae' and 'Discours' of Descartes' treatise on method also offer a critique of (traditional) metaphysics. Kant's critique of reason provides a basis for just the sort of maturity which appears to be of the very essence of the Enlightenment, and, in so far as it is, the aim of the Enlightenment and that of Kantian critique are one and the same: the autonomous agent. In Wittgenstein we search in vain for an attempt to establish the self-activity of reason and to justify maxims of action. The critique of language is not the critique of reason.[17]

But let us leave these aspects of exegesis and turn again to the main question: what grounds, what internal reasons are there which tell against a Kantian interpretation? I have in mind, in the first instance, one consideration: namely, the striking contrast on the one hand between Kant's idea that the conditions of experience, like their possibility, are *given a priori*, and, on the other hand, Wittgenstein's adamant empiricist conviction that no component of experience is *a priori*. All that we experience could also have been otherwise! In other words, and expressed in terms of Kant's criterion of the *a priori*: there is only *logical, and there is no empirical, necessity*. Wittgenstein seems to follow Mauthner, who replied to the neo-Kantian motto 'back to Kant' with his own: 'back to Hume'.

A similar conclusion can quite clearly be drawn from the notes on the concept of a cause, which were published by Rush Rhees in 1976.[18] From these it can be shown — and this is already known from the *Philosophical remarks* — that Wittgenstein is an intellectual successor of Oswald Spengler, and thus of Goethe, rather than of Kant. Supposing one wanted to know what the conditions are which lie at the basis of our understanding of the connection between cause and effect, then the question is not 'What is necessarily contained in any experience of such a connection?' and even less 'What is the condition of the possibility that A is the cause of B?', but the answer is rather a matter of turning to a simple case.

> The game 'finding the cause' exists, first of all, in a certain practice. First there must be a solid, hard stone with which to build, and the blocks will be placed, *unhewn*, one upon the other. *Then* it is of course important, that it can be hewn, that it isn't so hard after all. The primitive form of the language game is certainty, not uncertainty. For [and this argument seems significant to me] uncertainty could not lead to action.
>
> I want to say: it is characteristic of our language, that it grows on a basis of solid forms of life and regular activities.
>
> Its function is primarily determined through the action, whose accompanist it is.
>
> We even have an idea of which forms of life are primitive, and which can only arise out of these. We believe that the simpler plough came before the more complicated one.

For this reason it is also true that: 'The simplest form (the proto-type) of the cause-effect game is that of the determination of the cause, not that of doubt.'[19]

If we take up the challenge, with regard to this search for a simplest form and to this introduction of a praxeological dimension, to consider the language game as the primary thing, it becomes clear that the mysterious notion of a 'form or way of thinking' is just as praxeological; that is, it rests upon actual activity, and finally, upon the 'common way of human acting'.

Language games are only possible if one has confidence in something. But Wittgenstein clearly emphasises that this is not to mean 'if one can have confidence in something'.[20] What is being spoken of here is not a condition of possibility, but a purely factual condition — a fact.

The idea that recurring practices and habits, the praxeological basis of our cognitions, are constructed out of facts reappears in several passages: 'I mean: this is simply what we *do*. This is use and custom among us, or a fact of natural history' (RF I §63). This is not, for Wittgenstein, a transitory argument, leading us back to conditions of possibility, but a praxeological found-ationalism, which takes the fact of activity not as norm, but as the basis of cognition.

No one could be motivated to insinuate here that there was an indirect, much less direct, influence of the philosopher from Kön-igsberg on Wittgenstein. And yet the entirety of philosophy rests upon the same basis in both cases: the primacy of practical action over theoretical, or as Kant said, the primacy of practical reason.

The recurring reference to the *form* of thinking, to the possibil-ity of changing points of reference, to ways of thinking and the like serves after all not (as one might have us believe) to defend the position that the objects of experience are a projection of human reason, whose structure determines the structure of nature. It is rather the other way around: the facts of natural history — the development of human systems of activity — are the basis of our rational understanding in general.

The possibility of a change of perspective, to which Wittgen-stein repeatedly refers, is therefore neither a dogmatic nor a sceptical device but a methodological one — allowing one to imagine the course of history as other than it is. But we only find out *how* it is, when our cognition grasps where it finds hold: on the raw ground of the language in which we describe states of affairs.

Now there is indeed a possible perspective, which has been almost completely neglected in the foregoing investigation, and which would have offered a means to a more precise analysis of our question: the historical perspective. Such an approach might take as its point of departure the fact that towards the end of the nineteenth century and throughout the first quarter of this century there was a strong philosophical movement which attempted to provide transcendental foundations for a theory of science: neo-Kantianism. Of its two variants, the logical-scientific and the value-theoretic modes of criticism, the first showed some similarities to the positivist theory of science that stemmed from empiricism, since it was one of the principal intentions of the Marburg neo-Kantians to found a systematic science. They shared with Kant and positivism a rejection of metaphysics, but then, such coarse parallels can be drawn between just about any given two perspectives. This similarity, then, will not be a useful one. If one looks more closely at the central lines of thought of logical-scientific neo-Kantianism, one finds a more deeply-rooted metaphysics of history and historical construction than one might be led to expect from its starting question — how knowledge, or even awareness, of objects is at all possible. In the answer to this question, Kantian and yet venturing beyond Kant, the world of objects is represented as the correlate to a 'consciousness in general' whose task is to acquire knowledge as a value in itself. However, it is in making reason ethical that the greatest distance is created between Wittgenstein's praxeological foundationalism and the neo-Kantian position. The way in which the logical-mathematical form of representation of the thing-in-itself is expounded in neo-Kantianism is entirely different from how it is done by Wittgenstein. The objects of the *Tractatus* are not the points of connection of a synthesis, and the use of signs and of linguistic expressions is not the creation or constitution of a worldview. That which lies at the basis of a language game is neither a task nor a norm as it is for the neo-Kantians of both kinds, but rather something factual, like a habit.

It would be worthwhile to look into this in greater depth, although present space does not permit this here. I mention only that such a treatment would also show that the alleged similarity between Wittgenstein and Ernst Cassirer, the most eminent member of the Cohen School, is also conceived upon a misunderstanding of Wittgenstein's concept of language.

Notes

1. S. Cavell, 'The availability of Wittgenstein's later philosophy', *Philosophical Review* (1962), pp. 67-93.

2. I. Kant, *Prolegomena to any future metaphysics*, ed. L.W. Beck, (Bobbs-Merrill, New York, 1950), Appendix I, p. 123, note 2.

3. Cf. the following to J. Bouveresse, 'La notion de 'grammaire' chez le second Wittgenstein', in *Wittgenstein et le problème d'une philosophie de la science* (Edition du Centre National de la Recherche Scientifique, Paris, 1970), pp. 173-89.

4. P.M.S. Hacker, *Insight and illusion* (Oxford University Press, Oxford, 1972).

5. PG.

6. Ibid.

7. See Hacker, *Insight and illusion*, p. 00; S. Morris Engel, *Wittgenstein's doctrine of the tyranny of language* (M. Nijhoff, The Hague, 1971), pp. 45-73.

8. Cf. this difficult passage from the *Philosophical investigations* I, 372: 'The only correlate ...'

9. L. Wittgenstein, *Ludwig Wittgenstein and the Vienna Circle, conversations recorded by Friedrich Waismann*, trans. J. Schulte and B. McGuinness, (Basil Blackwell, Oxford, 1979), pp. 77-8.

10. Cf. R. Haller, 'The common behaviour of mankind'; Chapter 8 below.

11. Cf. ibid.

12. PG p. 00.

13. Hacker, *Insight and illusion*, p. 00.

14. Ibid., p. 00.

15. J.G. Hamann, *Sämtliche Werke*, ed. J. Nadler, (Herder, Vienna, 1949-57); F. Mauthner, *Beiträge zu einer Kritik der Sprache* (Cotta-Mundus, Stuttgart/Berlin, 1901-2); cf. G. Janoska, *Die sprachlichen Grundlagen der Philosophie* (Akademische Druck und Verlagsanstalt, Graz, 1951).

16. Cf. I. Kant, 'What is the Enlightenment?' in *Foundations of the metaphysics of morals*, trans. L.W. Beck, (Liberal Arts Press, New York, 1959).

17. Cf. Chapter 4 below.

18. L. Wittgenstein, 'Ursache und Wirkung: intuitives Erfassen', ('Cause and effect: intuitive awareness'), ed. R. Rhees, *Philosophia*, VI (1976), pp. 409-24; cf. Chapter 8 below.

19. Wittgenstein, 'Ursache und Wirkung: intuitives Erfassen', ('Cause and effect: intuitive awareness'), pp. 420-1.

20. OC §509.

4

Philosophy and the Critique of Language: Wittgenstein and Mauthner

In Ludwig Wittgenstein's logical-philosophical treatise, better known as the *Tractatus logico-philosophicus*, proposition number 4.0031 states: 'All philosophy is a "critique of language" (though not in Mauthner's sense).' Over the years, and particularly recently, this passage, like others in the *Tractatus*, has frequently been subject to discussion. Although a singular passage, in which an explanatory comment such as 'All philosophy is a "critique of language"'' appears, carries little logical weight within the main architecture of the *Tractatus*, constructed by its seven principal propositions, it is an *interpretandum* of some weight. A *terminus technicus*, as it were, is introduced here, a trademark for that which philosophy is or ought to be, and, in order to preclude misinterpretations, Mauthner's manner of doing philosophy is chosen to represent what it is not. As a result, Wittgenstein's interpreters have been compelled at least to acknowledge Mauthner's existence, and have thereby broken once again the undeserved silence over this ingenious dilettante. Wittgenstein placed the expression 'critique of language' in quotation marks, as though this expression was assumed to be well-known. What is then to be understood by '*critique* of language' and what role does it play *in* philosophy and *as* philosophy?

An inquiry into the idea's origin shows that the Wittgensteinian position, like that of Mauthner, can be placed in a wider context that allows us to view the history of a philosophical era from a better vantage point — an era that many believe culminated in a philosophical revolution. Whoever pursues this line of inquiry will, presumably, be able to avoid multiplying the errors committed in the numerous interpretations of the descriptivism in the *Philosophical investigations* which attribute a calculated moderation to the critical import of the investigations.[1] In such interpretations, it is as if Wittgenstein's programmatic announcement 'All philosophy is a "critique of language"' had lost itself in the vapours of the ordinary language of human communication.

Before coming to terms with this interpretative error I would like to return for a moment to the question of origins. To answer it appropriately, we must proceed from Mauthner's point of view, which we can assume was familiar to Wittgenstein. Fritz Mauthner, who said that he could have spared himself much trouble had he had informed counsel at his side at the right time,[2] stumbled, not quite accidentally, upon a long 'family history' of the critique of language; a family history which takes us back on one side through John Locke and Thomas Hobbes to the late-scholastic nominalists, and on the other, through Otto Friedrich Gruppe and Friedrich Jacobi to J.G. Herder, J.G. Hamann and G. Vico. There is an almost unbroken tradition of the critique of language, only hidden from time to time by changing public and academic interests, a tradition which Mauthner revived and for whose rediscovery in this century, at least in Gruppe's case, he is largely responsible.[3]

The tradition of using the critique of language as an instrument of philosophical analysis has an opponent in common with nominalistic criticism and with the later logical empiricism: metaphysical speculation. The tendency of speculative philosophy to become systematic philosophy led many critics of language to also criticise philosophical systems, or, as in Mauthner's case, to advocate scepticism, the exemplary form of which is found in the work of Hume. The call 'back to Kant' was rejoined by Mauthner's 'back to Hume'; Mauthner saw through the traditional empiricist stereotype; a stereotype, incidentally, which seems to have survived to this day:

> The German school of philosophy [so he says] has become used to regarding English common sense, which has made English philosophy so fruitful, as inferior; but where that common sense is paired with the utmost dauntlessness, as it is in Hume, it seems to me that its restriction to the psychological, its abstention from German metaphysics, is to the advantage of the English mind.[4]

I have maintained for some time the view that Austrian philosophy — if one may so christen a one-hundred-year-old tradition

— chose for its teachers not Kant and Hegel, but Mill and Hume, and that the principal figures in Austrian philosophy have remained 'mainly empiricist, and oriented towards science and the critique of language'.[5] For this reason it does not seem to me to be unwarranted to count Mauthner, who reached maturity in Bohemia, as a member of this tradition, in spite of the geographical directions in which his later life was to take him. William Johnston has also done so, in his recent, and very rich and comprehensive book on the Austrian mind.[6] However, this really serves only as a promissory note towards a full history of the critique of language, in which, for example, it would be just as important to include a chapter on Adolf Stöhr as a chapter on the various stages of the Brentano School.

Among the figures discussed in the first volume of Mauthner's *Towards a critique of language* (1901-2), we find Locke and Vico, Hamann and Jacobi. From Jacobi, Mauthner cites Hamann's catchphrase, that we lack no more than 'a critique of *language*, which could be a *meta-critique* of reason'. A revealing analogy is offered by this Jacobian thesis, which takes us a step towards the answer to our question about the critique of language. The critique of language should be, in a broad sense, a critique of knowledge and knowledge acquisition; not a critique of 'pure reason', but rather of language-dependent, and thus 'impure', reason, to use a phrase of Gustav Gerber's, whose *Die Sprache und das Erkennen* (1884) shows him to be among the most important of Mauthner's predecessors. 'Kant', Gerber reiterates a hundred years after Hamann, 'didn't submit language to a critique',[7] even though language is 'the sole, the first and last organon and criterion of reason', as it is strikingly put by the Magus of the North.

Nonetheless, if it is desirable to inquire into the possibility and capacity of the mind or of knowledge, then necessarily we must inquire into this sole organon as well. Mauthner never tired of pointing out that this instrument must be subjected to critique, because a human being has no reason apart from his language[8] and because language is 'unfit for knowledge of the world'.[9] Here we find a substantive, perhaps the substantive, result of Mauthner's 'epistemological nominalism'.

Mauthner's arguments for this thesis are diverse and if one retraces the pattern of inference, can be seen to be derived from several sets of premises. One of these sets is contained, for example, in the argument, motivated by empiricist-positivist lines of thought, that there can be nothing in the understanding which did not first appear to the senses; that is, that knowledge rests upon sensory elements. Ernst Mach, whom Mauthner proudly invokes, is the direct predecessor of this sort of sense data theory, and Bertrand Russell adopted a similar, if less phenomenological point of view, which he also ascribed to the early Wittgenstein through his interpretation of the *Tractatus*.[10] Nonetheless, Mauthner draws the decisive premises from the critique of language itself: First, 'language' is 'along with all of its most general formulations in logic and grammar, its expressions and hypotheses, ... a contingent phenomenon'.[11] 'The words of the language are ... unsuited to penetrating the nature of reality, because words are mere memory-tags for the sensations given by our senses, and because our senses are contingent, and in fact never experience more than the spider does of the palace in whose turret windows she has spun her web.'[12] One judges falsely when one assumes that language is the instrument of thought, because 'Thought is Speech', or 'Thought is speech reduced to its retail value.' As a result, truth is likewise not to be found in a relationship of agreement between a statement and a state of affairs or reality, but is merely 'to be sought in language'.[13] Not that Mauthner always remained consistent on this point. However, even when he does define truth as agreement with reality (as is usually done), he adds that reality is, in itself, nothing more than language. The deeper reason for this is to be seen in the fact that the variety of languages and uses of language express only the interests of the people who create and use them: 'Man has ordered the world in his language',[14] and because language submits to change with much more difficulty than does man, this order is often not nearly so useful as it could be.

> The categories of grammar, developed through the endless years of the history of language, and which the child learns in the form of a mother tongue within a few years, are really just an index of a world-catalogue which language strives to achieve; in a sense, the alphabet upon which the ultimate catalogue of the world will be ordered. It would be very unphilosophical to believe in the objectivity of this alphabet.[15]

In Mauthner's eyes any attempt to invent a 'world-cataloguing language' is, then, a utopian one; the pursuits of Raimundus Lullus, J. Wilkins or G.W. Leibniz were doomed to failure from the beginning.[16] Indeed, this would implicate the programme of the *Tractatus* as well, in so far as it proposes the use of a *symbolic language* to eliminate the 'elementary confusions' that arise so easily from ordinary usage. Anticipating Wittgenstein, Mauthner characterises logic as empty of content, as a system of tautologies. Though while Wittgenstein was of the persuasion that the sentences of ordinary language 'just as they stand, are in perfect logical order'[17] (admittedly for reasons that cannot be discussed here), Mauthner's critical inquiries into language had sceptical results: for him, the instrument — the language of our culture — is not only 'chewed away down to the bone',[18] but also remains, itself, a contingent artefact. A knowledge of the external world, of one's own and of another's mind is impossible, because only fleeting and ephemeral sensory experiences serve as the basis of our judgements, and we support ourselves and our 'verbal superstitions' upon mere chimeras and self-deceptions when we project our human and all-too-human concepts and categories upon nature. As a consequence, not only theological but also metaphysical and ontological expressions (in the narrow sense) are subject to critical dissection. 'We must return to Hume, in order to enter from there into fertile scepticism.'[19] When Mauthner speaks of the three worlds of language, the adjectivist world of common language, the substantivist world of metaphysics and the verbal world of science, it is primarily the substantivist and verbal worlds which fall victim to critical demystification. I recount one of many examples:

> ... there is nothing real that would correspond to the concept of the understanding. There is nothing real that would correspond to the concept of reason. And still less is there something real that would divide into two entities, understanding and reason. Just as little as there is a Beastness and two subtypes falling under it — Dogness and Catness.[20]

Mauthner persistently directs the anti-Platonic, de-reifying critique of metaphysics, which may appear to be only a consequence of a language-critical scepticism, against language itself. For, firstly, 'the language' which is the object of inquiry does not exist, not even as folk language. There is nothing over and above mere idiolects and, more precisely, usages of language. 'Language is however not an object to be employed [e.g. as a tool,

R.H.], it is not an object at all, it is nothing but its use. Language is the usage of language.'[21] And, secondly, it is — also as it presently exists — not a means to knowledge, and for this reason not a means for bridging the epistemological distance between thought and reality. But since a person possesses no reason other than his language, a critique of reason — which is to determine the conditions and boundaries of knowing — is only possible as critique of language. It cannot possibly change the world. Philosophy itself can desire nothing more 'than critical attention to language. Philosophy can do no more, with regard to the organism of language or of the human mind, than a doctor can for the physiological organism; it can observe attentively and give names to events.'[22] For Mauthner, philosophy cannot be a set of doctrines; it can only be the ill-fated attempt, doomed to failure, to say the unsayable. We must, then, according to his conception of philosophy, distinguish between two tasks: (a) the critique of all spurious concepts and (b) the suspension or 'suicide of language'! The one liberates us from 'horror at the absurd monster of language', the other leads to a resolute and final eschewal of the word, to a mystical experience: to silence. Wittgenstein drew a similar conclusion in formulating the seventh proposition of the *Tractatus*: 'What we cannot speak about we must pass over in silence.' And he called mystical that which cannot be expressed, that merely shows itself. As in Mauthner, the mystical is not a problem, or a riddle — for in the strict sense there are no unanswerable questions — rather, this is an experience, a feeling: 'Feeling the world as a limited whole.'[23] Wittgenstein's intention in the *Tractatus* was to draw a boundary for thought, and, given the language-critical intention, this could only mean that such a boundary could only be drawn in the language and that what lies beyond the boundary has no sense, but is, rather, nonsense. The thinking subject is, then, neither part of nor constitutive of the world, but is a borderline. 'The world is *my* world; this is manifest in the fact that the limits of *language* (of that language which alone I understand) mean the limits of my world.'[24] It is not self-evident to me that a substantially different concept of showing is emerging here, from that which distinguishes the sayable and expressible from what can only be shown. I shall come back to this presently.

Thirty years have passed since Wittgenstein's death. Although until his death nothing more had been published than the *Tractatus logico-philosophicus*, a dictionary for elementary schools, and a

1929 paper of lesser importance, there were always 'private publications' of notes, lecture manuscripts and oral deliveries, at least since the conversations with Friedrich Waismann and Moritz Schlick in the later twenties and somewhat more frequently after the 'return' to Cambridge. This explains the early and growing influence upon Anglo-Saxon philosophy, but also, naturally, that upon Schlick. Georg Henrik von Wright indicates, in one of the only trustworthy and informative biographies yet written, that the development of the 'Cambridge School', like that of Vienna Circle logical positivism, was influenced in just this way. It was called the Cambridge School even then, and contemporary opinion of the school is witnessed directly in several writings from the thirties: Ernest Nagel's 'Impressions and appraisals of analytic philosophy in Europe', and Max Black's 'Relations between logical positivism and the Cambridge School of Analysis', for example.[25]

Today we survey the development of analytic philosophy at greater remove and have become accustomed to seeing broad differences between Oxford linguistic analysis and neopositivism. We wonder now at finding the early papers on the so-called 'later' Wittgenstein treated as 'therapeutic positivism', as a minor branch of neopositivism or of the Vienna Circle.

The past thirty years have seen the publication not only of the principal work of Wittgenstein's later development — the *Philosophical investigations* — as well as a number of writings from the so-called transition period, but also preliminary studies to the *Tractatus*, sets of *Zettel* or notes, some of them bound together by theme and some of them thematically scattered; in short, according to the reports of the executors of the Nachlass, the most important of Wittgenstein's writings have been published here. During the same period the secondary literature on Wittgenstein has grown considerably and has perhaps already become too vast to survey, as happens when a bibliography reaches more than sixty or seventy pages.[26] Since the publication of the *Schriften* (complete works) by Suhrkamp, German philosophy has discovered an interest in Wittgenstein and extended the secondary literature by making its own contributions (I am thinking of E.K. Specht, W. Stegmüller, A. Müller, W. Schulz, E. von Savigny, and K. Wuchterl)[27] as well as by translating some of the English literature on Wittgenstein.[28]

During the past thirty years some basic patterns in the interpretation of Wittgenstein's principal works, the *Tractatus* and the

Philosophical investigations, have emerged. Connections to the work of Frege, Russell, and Hertz on the one hand and to that of Kant and Schopenhauer on the other have played a substantial role for the interpreters of the *Tractatus,* just as connections to the positions of Socrates/Plato, Augustine, Descartes, Russell, Moore and the author of the *Tractatus* itself have been drawn on in the interpretation of the *Philosophical investigations.* The temporal proximity to the last has probably contributed to the tendency not to pursue other connections, and to view the peculiarity of the *Tractatus,* and that of the *Philosophical investigations,* as mutually exclusive. Wittgenstein's philosophy was divided into two entirely different 'philosophemes'; resulting in the differentiation between Wittgenstein I and Wittgenstein II. Some authors, among them Stegmüller,[29] who concurs with Stenius and Pitcher, don't even address the question of whether there might exist a continuity between the logically perfect language and the analysis of the 'rough ground' of ordinary language. As Kant's awakening from the dogmatic slumber through the idea of critique revealed the difference between the pre-critical and the critical, a similar strict distinction is supposed to be made plain by the critique in the *Investigations* of certain positions in the *Tractatus.* However, the similarity to the Kantian turn is, to be frank, pretty remote, and historians of philosophy do not readily divide philosophers into irreconcilable halves, and especially not when both halves are in some agreement.

It ought not to be astonishing then that there is a rising tendency to question the strict division between Wittgenstein I and Wittgenstein II.[30] In my opinion the bridge which allows access to a unifying interpretation, aside from whatever reasons there are internal to the interpretive method for supporting the *unity thesis,* is to be found in the 1975 edition of the *Philosophical remarks.* I have come to believe that the thesis of strict incompatibility and discontinuity between the early and the later Wittgenstein is incorrect. There remains only the question of what has been or could be brought in support of the thesis, and how its negation can be defended.

A difficulty faces every interpreter here: the new and unfamiliar approaches to philosophical questions, the uses of examples as well as the general points of departure from which Wittgenstein discovers problems, have caused the greatest difficulties in understanding and interpreting him. I am referring here not to basic schemata of interpretation internal to systems, such as the claim that Wittgenstein was a nominalist, or its complement, that Wittgenstein was a realist. Such schematic interpretations are on the same level as the schemata of the realist or idealist interpretations of Kantian transcendentalism. They concern the ontological and metaphysical interpretation of a theory (using 'theory' in its broadest sense); that is, they address the question of what interpretation should be given to the status of individual signs *within* the system. By contrast, the basic difficulty is concerned with the perspective on the theory as a whole, and one could also say, with the *points of access to it*. It appears that some can find access only to the later *Investigations*, with its profusion of examples, and others only to the *Tractatus*. Russell and H. Scholz belong to the latter group, and Malcolm to the former.

If we consider what support can be found for the *discontinuity thesis*, we find there are already a number of well-supported arguments to be drawn from the standard interpretation:

1. The concept of a linguistic sign, as it is introduced in the *Tractatus*, is expanded in the later phase: signs are not bound to particular symbols. Speech is an activity, part of a 'form of life'.
2. The concept of the meaning of a linguistic sign is not the two-place semantical one of the *Tractatus* but is functionally or operationally determined by the rules of usage. 'The meaning of a word is its use in the language' (PI I §43). The definitions in the *Tractatus* are criticised. The meaning of a name is not the object. What an 'object' is, and its unity or simplicity, are not determined by the definition of the name.
3. Corresponding to the changes referred to in (1) and (2), the analysis of a *sentence* as a *mirror* of structure is expanded: there are different types of sentences, and not all have the same function, or even the same form. Type and form vary.
4. Language is not a unified system, not a sign language obedient to a special logical grammar. 'The philosophy of logic speaks of sentences and words in exactly the sense in which we speak of them in ordinary life.'[31] Even more clearly: 'all the propositions of our everyday language, just as they stand, are in perfect logical order'. The views of certain or even all logicians are too one-sidedly attached to one unrealised ideal in ordinary language.
5. As a result of (4), the concept of analysis is also expanded in the later phase; the narrow version of the *Tractatus* is criti-

cised. The idea of one and only one (complete) analysis of the proposition must be given up, since the elementary propositions cannot be the direct concatenation of names. 'We see that what we call "sentence" and "language" has not the formal unity that I imagined, but is the family of structures more or less related to one another' (PI I §108). Finally: 'The task of philosophy is not to create an ideal language, but to clarify the use of the existing language' (PI I §108).

If I perceive the matter correctly these are the gravest of the 'grave errors' attributed to the author of the *Tractatus* by the author of the *Philosophical investigations*. Hence I believe that it is an exaggeration to claim that there is in Wittgenstein some deadly ruthlessness, with which he is to have 'destroyed his entire earlier philosophy' and, thereby, to have attained an unparalleled uniqueness in the history of philosophy — and that such a claim is false. Certainly, Wittgenstein was ruthlessly honest, also with himself. Where others might have attempted to gloss over the inconsistencies in their systems, he tried to bring them to light, to express and to describe them. But Wittgenstein himself spoke only of grave errors, and nowhere indicated that he held his entire early philosophy to be mistaken. This hardly, if at all, lends support to the hypothesis that the later positions *eo ipso* destroyed the entirety of the earlier ones.

What evidence is there to support my view? Let us now return to those philosophers who regarded the development of Cambridge philosophy in light of logical empiricism, and who, as a result, interpreted Wittgenstein's 'new line of thought' as a continuation and modification of the Vienna Circle position. What reasons did they have, or better, might they have had, for maintaining such a reading? Wittgenstein himself clearly stated in the *Investigations* that he had been working on these issues for sixteen years — since 1929.[32] Pursuing this suggestion, it becomes evident that the clearest signs of a new beginning, those that appear in the *Philosophical remarks*, contain many of the basic thoughts and arguments of the later period, and some of these are less carefully formulated than those that we find in the *Investigations*. In the *Philosophical investigations*, Wittgenstein remarks: 'Grammar does not tell us how language must be constructed in order to fulfil its purpose, in order to have such-and-such an effect on human beings. It only describes and in no way explains the use of signs.'[33] And in several places in the same work, he characterises the manner of a philosophical investigation as non-hypothetical, non-empirical; in short, as grammatical. This thought is found in the *Tractatus*, where the necessity of introducing a sign language is treated, but in place of 'grammar', we read 'logical syntax',[34] as this is understood, for example, in Frege's *Begriffsschrift*. The interpretation of this syntax assigns to the sentence the function of picturing reality in such a way that the logical structure of the sentence isomorphically represents the structure of a state of affairs. The sentence *shows* its sense; that is, it shows what is the case when it is true. What it is to understand the sense of a sentence is stated in an oft-quoted passage from the *Tractatus*: 'To understand a proposition means to know what is the case if it is true' (TLP 4.024).

It has been supposed that this passage provides the earliest formulation of a verification criterion for the meanings of indicative sentences. However, if it is also correct to say that Wittgenstein sets up a relationship between the meaning of an indicative sentence and that which is the case when the sentence is true, it would still be wrong to assume that Wittgenstein would have identified meaning with the possibility of verification.

Judging from some remarks in a letter to Russell dated 19 August 1919,[35] Wittgenstein places the greatest value upon the clarification of the categorial difference between what can be *said* in the sentences of a language and what can only be *shown*. The sentence does not, however, *assert* a sense, but rather *shows* it, in that *if* one understands the sentence, one also knows what its truth conditions are or must be. On this basis, Wittgenstein arrived at his influential explication of logical propositions as meaningless propositions; meaningless because they have no relation of representation to reality, but rather leave open the entire infinite logical space — all possible states of affairs. The possibility that truth conditions might be exhibited, or that one could let them show themselves, also brings with it, for Wittgenstein, the possibility of letting the limits of language and the limits of the world fall together. Meaninglessness, and, if it differs in any respect, nonsense, commence at the limits.

Some of the philosophical remarks from the year 1930 sound like commentaries, when they state, for example:

But the essence of language is a picture of the essence of the world; and philosophy as custodian of grammar can in fact grasp the essence of the world, only not in the propositions of language, but in rules for this language which exclude nonsensical combinations of signs.[36]

What concatenations of signs must be excluded, according to this critical device? Again, Wittgenstein's answer is in accord with the postulate of verificationism: those strings of signs must be excluded whose truth or falsity are undecidable. But the thought-experiment of considering possible states of affairs is limited: it does not suffice to merely describe an experiment in order to produce a result; 'rather, the experiment must really be performed'.[37] Naturally, it is also possible to find something by aimless pursuit, or by chance. 'Then ... he wasn't looking for it, and the procedure, from the logical point of view, was synthetic; while seeking is an analytic process.'[38] That is, only where there is a problem, can a claim be justified. 'Whatever one can tackle is a problem' (TLP 6.51). One is reminded of the passage in the *Tractatus*, where it is stated that a question can only (properly) be asked where there is an answer, and the sort of answer that belongs to the class of 'what can be said' (PR p. 63).

But how does one ever know what is necessary for verification? One *expects* an event, and the expectation represents itself as a model of the event. The occurrence of the event corroborates the expectation. 'If you exclude the element of intention from language, its whole function then collapses.'[39] The testing, confirmation or invalidation of a hypothesis takes place *within* a system, in which the arguments brought for or against the hypothesis originate. What, however, corroborates an hypothesis? In *On certainty*, written in the last year of his life, Wittgenstein writes: 'What counts as an adequate test of a statement belongs to logic. It belongs to the description of the language game.'[40] The assertion that a statement must be true or false does not yet imply anything about *how* a statement is to be verified, it implies only that 'it must be possible to decide for or against it (the proposition)'.[41]

How we can, in fact, test what we say depends upon the function of the language game; that is, it depends primarily upon whether the corresponding sentence describes, explains, predicts or questions — in short, how it is used. That it can be tested in various ways *shows* that it has various meanings. The *Philosophical investigations* demonstrates that there is a variety of testing procedures for linguistic expressions. Only in use does meaning show itself, just as a result is only provided by a real experiment.

Wittgenstein's philosophy, therefore, began as and remained a critique of language. The important conclusions that philosophy as critique of language has to offer us remain unchanged in the course of his work. That philosophy is not a set of doctrines but an activity; that philosophical results are not found in 'philosophical propositions' but in making propositions clear; that philosophy is not a natural science and does not proceed hypothetico-empirically; these credos, already conceived in the *Tractatus*, not only remain exempt from self-criticism, but are also repeated in the later phase, in different variations. The change in perspective concerns the evaluation of the possibility and fruitfulness of constructing an ideal sign language which would preclude the errors of ordinary language. Here Wittgenstein manifests not only a growing scepticism with regard to the idea of the exactness of such languages, but also finds, in the poly-functionality of linguistic expressions, a deeper reason to deny that all descriptive expressions are uniform. The change of perspective leads to an investigation into the actual uses of the words of a language:

> When philosophers use a word — 'knowledge', 'being', 'object', 'I', 'proposition', 'name' — and try to grasp the *essence* of a thing, one always asks oneself: is the word ever actually used in this way in the language game which is its original home? What *we* do is to bring words back from their metaphysical to their everyday use. (PI I §116)

What is destroyed in bringing words back to their everyday use is not a deeper meaning, which one ought to be looking for behind the surfaces of linguistic utterances: 'All that we destroy are castles in the air' (PI I §118). For the sense of an expression depends upon the language game within which it appears. For this reason, it does not seem quite right to me to find an outright rejection of the 'language of the intellectuals' in this eliminative project, as Kuno Lorenz suggests in his otherwise intriguing portrayal of Wittgenstein's critique of language.[42] The point is not to eliminate or impose a taboo upon specialised languages, but to understand the constitution of the meaning of a text by way of *de facto* comprehensible usage. The conception of a language game has as its core concept that of meaning, which (contrary to a traditional interpretation of the notion of meaning) is determined by the function of an expression in a language game. Wittgenstein's polemic is thus directed against a misleading theory of meaning: the meaning of an expression is not a 'something', to which the expression stands in relation. Mauthner writes: 'Most people suffer from the intellectual weakness of believing that because a word is there, it must be for something; because the word is there, it must correspond to something real.'[43] Wittgenstein focuses this thought in the directive to inquire after use, not meaning. The sense of a proposition is 'not anything spiritual ... it's what is given as an answer to a request for an explanation of the sense.'[44] If the sense of a proposition is 'nothing spiritual' then it must be sought elsewhere.

For this we would need insight into the variety of human language games, language games that serve many different purposes. Philosophers — and theoretical linguists and historians of literature should not be excluded — nourish themselves on a lopsided diet and fail to notice that they are only making themselves ill. The representational and descriptive function of language is taken as basic and the diversity of language games is forgotten: commands, questions, recounting, idle talking, contriving stories, play-acting, telling riddles, requesting, thanking, swearing, greeting, praying, telling jokes, posing hypotheses and putting something to the test: these are all examples of practices that cannot be reduced to one basic practice. The act of *naming* is only one of these and is in no way primary. Wittgenstein rigorously focuses our attention upon the dangers of hasty and irresponsible generalising, a familiar phenomenon in the history of philosophy and thus in philosophy of language. There *is* no common form or essence underlying all language games; what there are, are at most similarities, different relations of resemblance between different activities. In bringing to our attention the multiplicity of linguistic performances, Wittgenstein recovers, for study in the philosophy of language and linguistic theory, ways of using language that have been banned, since Aristotle, for all but rhetoricians and poets.

The language-critical intention is primarily directed towards revealing, through description of usage, a misleading or misled *philosophical* usage, and thereby rendering it harmless. When Wittgenstein speaks of metaphysical usage, he refers to the philosophical, as opposed to the ordinary, usage. It would, however, be trivialising his intention to see in this an attempt to protect the latter from revision. To be sure, he says himself that 'philosophy leaves everything as it is'. But this only means that, as *critique of language*, philosophy is not a reformative undertaking but a descriptive one, which should show us when language is merely idling, and it means that the rules which contribute to the formation of the boundaries of language are sometimes violated. It would nonetheless be a crude error of interpretation to frame the activity of language-critical problem-solving as a systematic construction of an empirical theory. The verificationism summoned by Wittgenstein is indeed empiricist, in that it takes recourse to describable phenomena and not 'revelations'[45] as verifying instances. However, these instances lie within the competence of the speakers that have learned a language and are not to be explicated without incorporating them into the pragmatic dimension. The direction that a reconstruction of Wittgenstein's philosophy of language would have to take is indicated here. That is to say, we must bring in not only the linguistic context but also the non-linguistic context of the situation: the action, in the analysis of language and the understanding of language. Without the frame of reference of common human practices and behaviour, there is no possibility of interpreting any language at all. It appears to me that this composes the anthropological foundation of the critique of language: that in the beginning was not the word, but the deed.

Notes

1. Cf. Hans Albert, *Treatise on critical reason*, originally published as *Traktat über kritische Vernunft*. (J.C.B. Mohr, Tubingen, 1968), p. 145 (German edn).

2. Fritz Mauthner, 'Selbstdarstellung', in *Die Philosophie der Gegenwart in Selbstdarstellungen*, ed. R. Schmidt (F. Meiner, Leipzig, 1922), p. 133.

3. Fritz Mauthner, 'Otto Friedrich Gruppe', *Die Zukunft*, 5 (1913); cf. also H. Cloeren (ed.), *Philosophie als Sprachkritik im 19. Jahrhundert* (Fromann-Holzboog, Stuttgart-Bad Cannstatt, 1971).

4. Fritz Mauthner, *Wörterbuch der Philosophie* (2 vols, Munich 1910-11; 3 vols, Leipzig 1923-4), vol. II, p. 360.

5. Cf. ibid. ch. VI, p. 79; ch. VIII, p. 109.

6. William M. Johnston, *The Austrian mind. An intellectual and social history 1848-1938* (University of California Press, Berkeley-Los Angeles, 1972), p. 196ff.

7. Gustav Gerber, *Die Sprache und das Erkennen* (R. Gaertner, Berlin, 1884), p. 52; cf. also Cloeren (ed.), *Philosophie als Sprachkritik im 19. Jahrhundert*.

8. Fritz Mauthner, *Beiträge zu einer Kritik der Sprache* (3 vols, Cotta-Mundus, Stuttgart, 1901-2, vol. II, p. 495; cf. also the following: Gershon

Weiler, 'On Fritz Mauthner's "Critique of language"', *Mind*, 67 (1958), pp. 80ff; Elisabeth Leinfellner, 'Zur nominalistischen Begründung von Linguistik und Sprachphilosophie: Fritz Mauthner und Ludwig Wittgenstein', *Studium Generale*, 22 (1969), pp. 209-51.

9. Fritz Mauthner, vol. I, p. 216.

10. Cf. Bertrand Russell, 'Introduction' to the *Tractatus logico-philosophicus*, eds D.F. Pears & B.F. McGuinness (Humanities Press, Atlantic Highlands, 1974); James Griffin, *Wittgenstein's logical atomism* (Oxford University Press, London, 1964).

11. Mauthner, *Beiträge*, vol. III, p. 589.

12. Ibid., p. 19, p. 176.

13. Ibid., vol. I, p. 638.

14. Ibid., p. 73.

15. Ibid.

16. Cf. Rudolf Haller, 'Das "Zeichen" und die "Zeichenlehre" in der Philosophie der Neuzeit', *Archiv für Begriffsgeschichte*, 4 (1959), pp. 113-57.

17. TLP 5.5563.

18. Mauthner, *Beiträge*, vol. I, p. 215; cf. also the following: Mauthner, 'Selbstdarstellung', p. 135ff; and the short but very clear treatment by Gershon Weiler, 'On Fritz Mauthner's "Critique of Language"', *Mind*, 67 (1955).

19. Mauthner, 'Selbstdarstellung', p. 137.

20. Mauthner, *Beiträge*, vol. I, p. 588.

21. Ibid., p. 23.

22. Ibid., p. 648.

23. TLP 6.45.

24. Ibid., 5.62.

25. Ernest Nagel, 'Impressions and appraisals of analytic philosophy in Europe', *Journal of Philosophy*, 33 (1936), pp. 5-53, reprinted in E. Nagel, *Logic without metaphysics and other essays in the philosophy of science* (Glencoe, Ill. 1956). Max Black, 'Relations between logical positivism and the Cambridge School of Analysis', *Journal of Unified Science/Erkenntnis*, 8 (1939/40), pp. 24-35.

26. Ilona Borgis, *Index zu Wittgensteins 'Tractatus logico-philosophicus' und Wittgenstein-Bibliographie*, (Alber, Freiburg-Munich, 1958). K.T. Fann, *Wittgenstein's conception of philosophy* (Basil Blackwell, Oxford, 1969), Bibliography, pp. 113-78.

27. Ernst Konrad Specht, 'Die sprachphilosophischen und ontologischen Grundlagen im Spätwerk Ludwig Wittgensteins', *Kant-Studien*, 84 (1963); Wolfgang Stegmüller, *Hauptströmungen der Gegenwartsphilosophie*, 4th edn (Stuttgart, 1969); Anselm Müller, *Ontologie in Wittgensteins Tractatus*, (Bouvier, Bonn, 1967); Walter Schulz, *Wittgenstein. Die Negation der Philosophie* (Neske, Pfullingen, 1967); Eike von Savigny, *Die Philosophie der normalen Sprache*, (Alber, Freiburg-Munich, 1969); Kurl Wuchterl, *Struktur und Sprachspiel bei Wittgenstein*, (Suhrkamp, Frankfurt, 1969).

28. Justus Hartnack, *Wittgenstein and modern philosophy*, (Doubleday, New York, 1969); George Pitcher, *The Philosophy of Wittgenstein* (Prentice Hall, Englewood Cliffs, N.J., 1964), trans. 1967; Erik Stenius, *Wittgenstein's Tractatus*, (Blackwell, Oxford, 1960), trans. 1969; David Pears, *Ludwig Wittgenstein*, (Fontana, London, 1971), trans. 1971.

29. Stegmüller, *Hauptströmungen der Gegenwartsphilosophie*; cf. Wolfgang Stegmüller, 'Ludwig Wittgenstein als Ontologe, Isomorphietheoretiker, Transzendentalphilosoph und Konstruktivist', *Philosophische Rundschau*, 13 (1965), pp. 116-52.

30. Rüdiger Bubner, 'Die Einheit in Wittgensteins Wandlungen', *Philosophische Rundschau*, 15 (1968). Cf. also Kuno Lorenz, *Elemente der Sprachkritik* (Suhrkamp, Frankfurt, 1970).

36. Wittgenstein, *Philosophical grammar*, ed. R. Rhees, trans. A. Kenny (Oxford University Press, Oxford, 1969), VI, p. 115.

32. PI, preface.

33. PI, I §496.

34. TLP 3.325.

35. As cited in G.E.M. Anscombe, *An introduction to Wittgenstein's Tractatus* (Hutchinson, London, 1959), p. 161.

36. PR p. 85.

37. Ibid., p. 152. Cf. Max Black, 'Verifications and Wittgenstein's reflections on mathematics', in C.G. Granger (ed.), *Wittgenstein et le problème d'une philosophie de la science* (Paris, 1970), pp. 138ff.

38. PR p. 16.

39. Ibid., p. 177.

40. OC §82; cf. also R. Haller, 'Concerning the so-called Münchhausen-Trilemma', *Ratio*, 16 (1974), pp. 125-40.

41. OC §200.

42. Lorenz, *Elemente der Sprachkritik*, pp. 113, 123; cf. also Pears, *Ludwig Wittgenstein*, pp. 120ff.

43. Mauthner, vol. 1, pp. 158ff.

44. PG p. 131.

45. OC §172.

5

Was Wittgenstein Influenced by Spengler?[1]

Initially the question of whether Wittgenstein was influenced by Spengler seems far less appropriate than that of whether Wittgenstein was a neo-Kantian.[2] After all, Wittgenstein's preoccupation with Schopenhauer — whose work visibly displays the principal themes of Kant's philosophy — is apparent from his earliest notes onwards. Moreover, Kant's name comes up repeatedly in Wittgenstein's writings, and there are several striking remarks that might encourage such an interpretation. However, this is hardly true in Spengler's case.

It would, therefore, be appropriate to begin by giving a brief sketch of a paper[3] that I first published some years ago on Spengler's influence upon Wittgenstein. The paper is concerned with Wittgenstein's position, completely neglected in the secondary literature, on the philosophy and methodology of Oswald Spengler, and more precisely, with the question of the actual influence exerted upon Wittgenstein's philosophical development by the work of this philosophical dilettante.

To begin with, it should be pointed out that until the discovery of the notes that are now collected in the *Vermischte Bemerkungen*,* no one would have associated Wittgenstein with Spengler in any way, much less imagined an intellectual bond between the author of the *Decline of the West* and the author of the *Tractatus logico-philosophicus*. Indeed, no one has ever made such a suggestion. This not only demonstrates a lack of imagination among philosophers and interpreters, but also indicates how remote, misplaced or even abstruse such an association would have

---

* *Vermischte Bemerkungen*, literally translated as 'miscellaneous remarks', is published in English under the title *Culture and value* [Tr.].

seemed. Even in a work that counts among its tasks the reconstruction of the currents of the *Zeitgeist* that influenced Wittgenstein and makes references to his admiration for Oswald
Spengler's *The Decline of the West*,[4] mention of the association is
confined to a half-sentence. It simply didn't occur to Janik and
Toulmin[5] to infer the existence of an *influence*, much less an
important influence, from Wittgenstein's acknowledged admiration for Spengler. Most would consider it unwarranted to even
speculate upon such a possibility.

It was the editor of the *Vermischte Bemerkungen* who, more than
anyone else, noticed the striking character of Wittgenstein's
unexpected admiration for Spengler. But von Wright found the
influence to be located, more than anywhere else, in a general
ideological pessimism. And this with evident good reason, for
both philosophers appear to have agreed on some essential points
in their judgements of the intellectual situation of the time. Thus
von Wright is sincere in asking whether we may say that Spengler
directly influenced Wittgenstein's perspective on life or whether
we ought rather to say that he corroborated it, and von Wright
refers here to Wittgenstein's 'contempt for the civilization of his
time', and to his prophetic assertions that the culture of the foregoing era, viz. the culture of the first decades of this century,
would end in ashes and ruins. In such an age of 'unculture',
humanity loses many of the qualities that characterise a culture,
as men pursue 'purely private ends' (CV p. 6). If one is at all
aware that Wittgenstein was influenced by the author of the *Decline*, then it is reasonable to assume that his rejection of belief in
progress may have been fortified by Spengler. Wittgenstein
imagined, then, that the apocalyptic vision of the course of world
history was a very real possibility, and that the course of world
events may not repeat itself.

> It isn't absurd, e.g., to believe that the age of science and
> technology is the beginning of the end for humanity; that
> the idea of great progress is a delusion, along with the idea
> that the truth will ultimately be known; that there is noth-
> ing good or desirable about scientific knowledge and that
> mankind, in seeking it, is falling into a trap. It is by no
> means obvious that this is not how things are. (CV p. 56)

The remark that 'It is by no means obvious that this is not how
things are' betrays Wittgenstein's actual position. For Wittgen-

stein, science brings enrichment *as well as* impoverishment (CV p. 60) and he makes clear his conviction that 'any speculation about a coming collapse of science is, for the present and for a long time to come, nothing but a dream'. Beneath the 'for the present' lies the opinion that the dream will become reality; not now, but certainly later.

> The spirit of this civilization makes itself manifest in the industry, architecture and music of our time, in its fascism and socialism, and it is alien and uncongenial to the author. (CV p. 6)

In the sketch of a preface to the *Philosophical remarks* Wittgenstein clearly counts himself among the many *Kulturkritiker* close to Spengler, who, building upon the opposition between culture and civilisation, fall upon the civilisation of western Europe with Nietzschean ridicule.

Wittgenstein's contempt for this form of life, and his preference for the traditional one, become clearly visible against the background of this opposition, although he hadn't wanted to pass *any* value judgements at all. There is, however, no question that the two thinkers met in their evaluations of the intellectual and spiritual situation of the time! And there is a certain dubious quality about this agreement. Why? Primarily because Spengler's judgements on the development of European culture within the course of the world's culture are, to a large extent, simply false, and not only false, but also fantastic, misled by emotion and provincialism, as may be inferred from the early satires of Spengler's work, written and published by Otto Neurath and Leonard Nelson, among others.[6]

I should note, parenthetically, that Schlick, who, with Waismann was closest to Wittgenstein of all in the Vienna Circle, raised sharp objections to Spengler's views: 'Spengler's philosophy will not last; it will be brought to ruin by its intellectual superficiality, which without critical self-awareness, arrogantly spins off an ephemeral *aperçu* as though it were a meaningful truth'.[7] In other contexts he speaks of the limitations of Spenglerian philosophising, and of its lack of dispassionate and clear judgement. In connection with Spengler's dispute with Darwin and the theory of evolution, Schlick remarks: 'The true philosopher need not disturb science in order to acquire a place for his own thoughts; for him there are no disturbing truths — science is

for him a self-evident assumption'.[8] While these criticisms by
Schlick were published only after his death, Neurath's opinion
had already been published by the time the Vienna Circle began
to meet. In his ruthless criticism of Spengler, Neurath also shows
himself to be one of the Vienna Circle's sharpest critics of Wittgenstein.[9]

As Wittgenstein was reading Spengler and beginning to take
him seriously, there were correspondingly earnest attempts made
by rationalist philosophers to expose this 'spook', and in particular, to challenge not only the inadequate basis of the Spenglerian
hypothesis, but also its systematically unjustified predictive
power. It was not the concern of these philosophers to refute the
claim that Europe had become old, and ripe for the decline of the
epoch. Neurath and Nelson were concerned, above all, to explic-
ate (and thereby indict) the Spenglerian *method* of representing
facts, his method of interpreting them, and his reckless production of forecasts, which they openly ridiculed. Their examples
were, of course, drawn from the work being criticised. Anyone
who has peered into the Aladdin's cave of the *Decline* will recall
that the analysis begins with a portrayal of mathematics intended
to support the claim that every science is constituted, shaped and
formed to a large extent by the fundamental currents of a given
culture or form of culture. Thus there is no (linear) history of
mathematics; there are only common forms of mathematical
thought: Egyptian, Greek and Faustian mathematics. The structures that outwardly appear to remain the same are also placed in
new contexts by the shifting of Gestalts; their roles in the system
are thereby subsumed under new rules.

This idea, along with countless others, was attacked. The
necessity of a given system, technique or form of proof for
conceptual relations cannot be derived from historical origins,
nor can an elevation of 'Faustian', that is, western mathematics in
preference to other forms, but these are questions that I cannot
address here.

Wittgenstein, as I have already mentioned, read Spengler. He
didn't cite him. And yet he included his name on a list — a list
that is, in my opinion, complete — of all those people whose
influence upon him was worthy of consideration. Most of the
names on this list — Boltzmann, Hertz, Schopenhauer, Frege,
Russell, Kraus, Loos, Weininger, Spengler, Sraffa — also appear
in his writings in forewords as well as in remarks elsewhere.
Spengler, the author of a widely-acclaimed text, remains among

those who are neither mentioned nor considered. Why might this be? Certainly not merely in order to establish agreement with existing opinion. For we must remind ourselves that Wittgenstein was quite tormented, in 1931, by the parasitic nature of his thought. ('I don't believe I have ever *invented* a line of thinking, I have always taken one over from someone else' (CV p. 19).)

It is within this context that Spengler and Sraffa are to be counted among those who were (chronologically) the last to influence him. Sraffa's influence is known from the preface to the *Philosophical investigations*, and from the various memoirs written about Wittgenstein. No one knew of his connections with Spengler.

This connection, if we take seriously the distressed remark above, would have to lead back to an *original* and independent *line of thinking*, engendered by Spengler and reproduced by Wittgensein. Of course, Wittgenstein not only reproduced, but also brought to the surface of clarity, the aspects of that line of thinking which most fascinated him. What was this 'line of thinking'? It is clear that there must be more to what Wittgenstein calls here a 'line of thinking' than a provocative or stimulating suggestion, or the adoption of a concept. Today we know that Frege's entire conception of logic was adopted by Wittgenstein during the writing of the *Tractatus*, and that Wittgenstein himself observed a close relationship between his own writing style and that of Frege. We also know, not least due to Janik, that Wittgenstein largely owes his conception of the relationship between logic and ethics to Otto Weininger, and that the latter's best seller *Sex and character*, exercised a stronger influence upon Wittgenstein than many of the great thinkers in the history of philosophy.[10] We may thus surmise that more than simply a concept, such as that of family resemblances, was taken from Spengler too. What then, was this line of thinking? This is our principal question, and my answer to it must be this: not the *content* of Spengler's analyses, though Wittgenstein may have happened to agree with many of them, but their *method* — led by the idea of a 'Gestalt lore' or 'Gestalt analysis' of history.

The method of descriptive morphology is brought into opposition with the inappropriate application of the methods of natural science to philosophical problems. In the introduction to the *Decline*, Spengler writes of Goethe's comparison of the world as mechanism with the world as organism, of a dead and a living nature, of form (Gestalt) and law as the eternal determinative principles, which are to be grasped only at great depths and which are completely hidden from the prejudiced viewer. 'Sympathy, contemplation, analogy, direct inner certainty, precise visual fantasy — these were his [Goethe's, R.H.] means of approach to the secret of the fleeting appearance. *And these are the means for the study of history in general.* There are no others.'[11] These are, moreover, Spengler's devices. Everything is revealed through comparison. This is why Spengler can say: 'The means for acquiring knowledge of the dead form is the mathematical law. The means for understanding the living form is the analogy.'[12] The procedure for comparative research is to determine the archetypal forms taken by the passage of history, and to derive from them — *per analogiam* — statements that render the future predictable. Of course, these would not be the kinds of predictions that forecast the appearance of certain individual figures or the occurrence of particular events, but rather foretell the direction to be taken by the development of history: these are the content of morphological prognosis.

Spengler's meta-theory interprets all historical events, in contrast to causal or mechanical events, as organic.

> Cultures are organisms. World history is her complete biography ... Should one want to acquaint oneself with the inner forms repeated everywhere, the comparative morphology of plants and animals has already prepared the method. The fate of the individual cultures, following upon one another, growing up next to each other, coming into contact with each other, overshadowing and overwhelming each other, exhausts the content of all human history. And if one lets these figures, which until now have remained all too deeply hidden under the surface of a 'History 'of Mankind' making its trivial way, parade before the mind, one ought also to be able to discover the original form of all culture, which lies at the basis of all individual cultures, free of cloudiness and insignificances. (*Decline*, pp. 140ff (German edn))

While the structural, morphological similarities between organs are understood in the homological respect, the analogical treatment is concerned with similarities between organic functions. But naturally, Spengler gives us no precise criteria for how homologies and analogies are to be ascertained in detail, as

Neurath and, at even greater length, Nelson have indicated.[13]

'But then how is a view like Spengler's related to mine?' Wittgenstein asks in 1937, after devoting more than a negligible amount of thought to this author for several years. And his answer does not adopt the critical, deprecating tone that characterises Neurath's and Schlick's remarks on Spengler. Wittgenstein finds in Spengler not only an intellectual kinsman, who declares his alienation from the surrounding civilisation, with its symptoms of a declining epoch, but also the initiator of an approach or 'line of thinking' which seems to him most appropriate as the methodological tool for the investigation of language games.

In this connection, Wittgenstein makes the following suggestion: 'Don't take comparability, but rather incomparability, as a matter of course.'[14] That is, in order to compare two phenomena with each other at all, there is need for some principle that justifies the comparison. In fact, Wittgenstein counts among his most important methods the imagining of 'a historical development for our ideas different from what actually occurred'.[15] In order to do this, he believes, one must depart from the usual presuppositions about causality which lead one to say 'so it must be', and break through to that domain of possibilities where a variety of potential realisations hold equal sway.

In order to bring the incomparable or unique in an event or phenomenon into comparative relation with another event or phenomenon, there is need for a frame of reference, expressed in a principle or method, which will regulate its application. Thus, for example, Christian von Ehrenfels suggested principles of comparability for gauging the Gestalt-level and the Gestalt-purity, though he only sketchily developed the method of their application.

Where the principle of Gestalt-level determines that the level of a given Gestalt is dependent upon the product of its constituent parts, its unity and the variety of its parts, the suggested means for comparing the Gestalt-levels would be stated thus: 'One imagines to oneself that the objects in question (a rose, and a heap of sand) are dismantled step by step in an accidental, irregular fashion. Whichever of the two objects survives the longer series of changes, this is a Gestalt of higher level.'[16] What is interesting here is that where what is expected is a method that sets down a canonical rule of variation, what is actually suggested is, rather, an arbitrary selection as a means to the achievement of objectivity

— a procedure which, of course, opposes that of causal explanation.

Wittgenstein's quasi-publication of 1933/34 — namely, the copies of the so-called *Blue book* (the first 'publication' to be released after 1929) — was primarily concerned with discovering what might hinder, or pose difficulties for, his preferred method for the investigation of simple language games. Simple language games are models of primitive linguistic forms or primitive languages, which allow for investigation free of the background of complex processes that appear in normal linguistic usage. He indicates that 'our striving for generality' is the main hindrance to the application of such a method of investigation. He expressively identifies 'the prejudice for the method of the natural sciences' as the principal cause of that striving. This prejudice, which leads the philosopher to generalise and to claim universal validity for philosophical propositions, also lends credibility to the assumption that any particular case can be subsumed under general laws. Just this 'contemptuous attitude towards the particular case' is to be eliminated through the critique of language.

> Philosophers constantly see the method of science before their eyes, and are irresistibly tempted to ask and answer questions in the way science does. This tendency is the real source of metaphysics, and leads the philosopher into complete darkness.[17]

This theme recurs in Wittgenstein's writing; the polarisation of philosophy and the natural sciences is, after the *Tractatus*, the key to the understanding of his method, which is clearly opposed to any naturalistic attempts at a unified science, seamlessly connecting physics with philosophy.[18] The philosopher's fixation upon *one* method could be likened, on the one hand, to the preference for a measuring rod that functions as a rule of measure *par excellence*, and on the other with a fixation upon *one* style that prevents us from giving our full attention to any other, when it is important to view the diversity of appearances as a diversity of individual phenomena. The subsumption of particular phenomena under a general one robs them of their context, a context that also determines the comparability and incomparability or uniqueness of types. 'Meaning is a physiognomy', Wittgenstein notes in one passage.[19] And physiognomies are accessible from many different standpoints. Perspectives, rules of measure, and styles are overarching forms that are used in order to see the particular thing for what it is. Thus the precaution: 'don't think, but look!'[20] According to Wittgenstein, it is just this tendency to prefer the causal-scientific way of thinking that is responsible for the fact that those philosophers who are attracted to this position look for explanations where they should be looking for descriptions.

'Our mistake is to look for an explanation where we ought to look at what happens as a "proto-phenomenon". That is, where we ought to have said: *this language game is played.*'[21] Such 'ultimate' or basic facts are used in a similar way in epistemic justifications as they are used in accordance with the morphological point of view, which focuses the attention upon the structural similarities between like and unlike types. The particular case should always be regarded as a *proprium*.

Spengler found that the existence of the particular first becomes meaningful through comparison, and that one must differentiate between the causal, natural-scientific aspect of an event and the destiny-aspect. The destiny-aspect comprehends the genius, the 'utterly common formative force', of the particular. 'Every culture', we read in the *Decline*,

> possesses a wholly unique way of seeing the world as nature or of becoming acquainted with it, or (what comes to the same thing) it has its own, peculiar 'Nature', which no other sort of man can possess in exactly the same form ... But in a far greater degree still, every Culture — including the individuals comprising it ... possesses a specific and peculiar sort of history, and it is in the picture of this and the style of this that the general and the personal, the inner and the outer, the world-historical and the biographical becoming, are immediately perceived, felt and lived. (*Decline*, p. 131)

In just this *im*precise sense, Spengler attributes to culture as 'proto-phenomenon' a *causal* and a destiny-aspect, where this is to mean that 'necessarily, every culture' must possess 'its own idea of its Destiny', which does not admit of further description.

> But destiny is the word for an inner certainty that is *not* describable. We bring out that which is in the causal by means of a physical or an epistemological system, through numbers, by reasoned classification; but the idea of destiny

can be imparted only by the artist working through media like portraiture, tragedy and music. The one requires us to *distinguish* and in distinguishing to dissect and destroy, whereas the other is *creative* through and through. (*Decline* p. 118)

And in Wittgenstein, we find it stated that: 'Fate is the antithesis of natural law. A natural law is something you try to fathom and make use of, but not fate.'[22] Here, the Cartesian notion of a foundation for all knowledge of which human understanding is capable is brought into direct relation with the utility and applicability of knowledge, while submission to existence here and now (*Dasein*) is taken to be implied by the notion of Fate. This notion of fated existence leads into Wittgenstein's concept of *form of life*, which represents the hard ground, the activity, out of which language grows. From the perspective of one way of acting and thinking, a person, facing an unpleasant event, is led to ask 'Who's to blame?' and thereby to seek to establish a connection to some *causa efficiens*; in another way of life, the passing of events is regarded as somehow destined, and the events are seen as something to which one must submit or accommodate oneself. It would, however, be an error to assume that such surrender is necessarily quietistic surrender.

A man reacts *like this*: he says 'No, I won't tolerate that!' — and then resists it. Perhaps this brings about an equally intolerable situation and perhaps by then strength for any further revolt is exhausted. People say: 'If he hadn't done *that*, the evil would have been avoided.' But what justifies this? Who knows the laws according to which society develops? I am quite sure they are a closed book even to the cleverest of men. If you fight, you fight. If you hope, you hope.

You can fight, hope and even believe without believing scientifically. (CV p. 60)

A passage in the *Decline* reads: '... the scholar of the abstract, the researcher of nature, the thinker of systems, whose entire intellectual existence is grounded upon the principle of causality, is a recent appearance of the unconscious hate for the powers of fate and the inconceivable'. Finally, in the same passage, fate is referred to as 'the actual mode of existence [*Dasein*] of the proto-phenomenon', in which the dynamic idea of Becoming directly unfolds itself. By contrast, from the causal theorist's perspective, all that is *felt* by the artist to be determinative is given no more status than that of mere 'goals in life'.

> Teleology is a caricature of the Destiny-idea ... It is the deepest and most characteristic tendency both of Darwinism — the megapolitan-intellectual product of the most abstract of all civilizations — and of the materialist conception of history which springs from the same root as Darwinism and, like it, kills all that is organic and fateful. Thus the morphological element of Destiny is an *Idea*, an idea that is incapable of being 'cognized', described or defined, and can only be felt and inwardly lived. This idea is something of which one is either entirely ignorant or ... entirely certain. (*Decline*, pp. 120-1)

What, one may ask, do the later developments in Wittgenstein's views have in common with such confused notions? However agreeable or disagreeable this may be for the reader, there is considerably more in common than is generally thought. Wittgenstein adopts the main principle of comparative morphology — but he uses it in such a way that no one would have thought of tracing it back to Spengler. He is also clearly aware of this himself. He reproaches Spengler for repeatedly making the mistake of extending the scope of statements true of the archetype of contemplation to the objects of contemplation.

Every language game (this is, in a certain respect, the contextual concept for Wittgenstein) can also be used as a model of comparison. But when one describes a language game as an archetype, then one is not permitted to contaminate the description with the object of description. Wittgenstein believed that Spengler would have made himself better understood if he had elucidated the comparison of different cultural periods in terms of the concept of *family resemblances*. Here, Wittgenstein wanted to say that the dominant concept of substance had to be 'weakened' for the purpose of elucidation. Resemblances are always relative resemblances, or kinship in a particular respect. This must be indicated, that is, the object of comparison must stand fast, so that the resemblances can be studied. The same holds for showing a mistake: 'If I rectify a philosophical mistake and say, one always imagined it this way, but it is not so ... so I must always show an analogy that has always been thought, but never acknowledged as an analogy.'

The concept of an archetype, like that of the proto-pheno-menon, is taken, as Spengler always emphasised, from Goethe's morphology. All ways of conceiving the world are kinds of morphology: but there are two principal kinds:

> The Morphology of the mechanical and the extended, a science which discovers and orders natural laws and causal relations, is called Systematic. The Morphology of the organic, of history and life and all that bears the sign of direction and destiny, is called Physiognomic. (*Decline*, p. 100)

But behind the systematic lies the physiognomy of a person in a culture. For Spengler, therefore, the science of physiognomy has to do with a sort of self-knowledge. The foreign cannot be fully grasped, for it is foreign to us, and here the notion of incommensurability comes to mind.

For Wittgenstein, this concept possesses a similar, though systematically regarded, completely different, meaning. He had also said that one must imagine the course of events quite differently than it actually is, if one is to know them in their particularity; and he also held that it is the primitive picture, rather than the complicated one, which is the prototype. For example, while it holds for the Marxian method that the anatomy of the human being provides a key to the anatomy of the ape, and therefore that the complicated form may be projected onto the simpler form, Wittgenstein suggests the reverse. Not that this should be taken as expressing a preference for a genetic perspective, since that would entail falling back upon the form of explanation used in the natural sciences. Rather, this form of investigation is to be understood, as in linguistic phenomenology, as a kind of *conceptual* investigation. And this tells us that the simple form comes before the complex one; that the simplest plough came before the complicated plough; that the simple language game comes before the complex language game. When we delineate a phenomenon as an archetype, therefore, it will serve as a basic idea from which to proceed, as a methodic device that determines an entire way of viewing the world, as a paradigm that can be laid alongside other objects as a measure. But this means that what can be predicated of the archetype itself, which determines our way of viewing things, cannot also be predicated of its objects. Moreover, it is precisely this relativisation of the concept of an archetype that frees Wittgenstein from accusations of relativism. He did not want to espouse a dogmatism of a destined *idea*, as Spengler did. Rather, he defended a foundationalism within a perspectivism. The archetype is not understood as a judgement, nor as an *idea* that is beyond intellectual grasp, but as a principle of the conceptualisation of objects, whose *utility* decides its suitability. Hence this foundationalism reveals itself as a pragmatic one, to be gauged in the actions of human beings. For this reason, I have referred to it elsewhere (in Chapter 3) as 'praxeological foundationalism'.

And so I return to my introductory thoughts: when we pose the question of how we are to justify our epistemic attitudes of belief, held with respect to 'truth' and 'knowledge', a series of justifications may be given which, in the case of knowledge, include truth and certainty. I have knowledge of a certain state of affairs if and only if the judgement that expresses it is true, and I have sufficient justification for it. However, since in judging I stand upon the foundation of my language, every foreign language poses a barrier to my understanding. But if I turn my attention to actions, I am shown the ultimate foundation — the foundation also of knowledge — in the shared practices of human beings. Wittgenstein's ambivalence towards the scientific worldview, a result of his acceptance of a dualism between saying and showing, and a dualism between science and philosophy, also has consequences for the morphologically-interpreted history of the world.

In the *Vermischten Bermerkungen* (*Culture and value*), a 1948 entry states: 'I may find scientific questions interesting, but they never really grip me. Only *conceptual* and *aesthetic* questions do that. At bottom I am indifferent to the solution of scientific problems; but not the other sort' (CV p. 79e). Among these 'other' questions we find not only the spells cast upon our understanding by linguistic confusions, but also, in equal measure, those problems of life of which Wittgenstein remarked in the *Tractatus* that they would remain untouched even were every *possible* scientific question answered. For one of his mind, enlightenment in the form of a unified science is neither possible nor desirable.

Both Spengler and Wittgenstein see a hiatus between the questions of science and the questions of philosophy or of history. If the former are determined by the ideal of the purely mechanical, and demand causal explanations as answers, then the latter are determined on the model of the painting of a picture, or the giving of a description. While the question of formal structure is no longer a pressing one in the construction of causal explanations, since a basic argument form has already been provided (in the Second Analytic) for causal explanations, the study of the perspectives from which objects are seen, pictured, or described remains important. 'What is important about depicting anomalies precisely? If you cannot do it, that shows that you do not know your way around the concepts.'[23]

In the *Philosophical investigations*, Wittgenstein even raises the question of whether the emphasis upon the concept of a *perspicuous representation* — 'our form of representing' — isn't actually a *worldview*.[24] Naturally, it is a worldview opposed to the scientific one:

> Philosophy simply puts everything before us, and neither explains nor deduces anything. — Since everything lies open to view there is nothing to explain. For what is hidden, for example, is of no interest to us. One might also give the name 'philosophy' to what is possible *before* all new discoveries and inventions.[25]

To arrive at clarity in aesthetic and ethical matters, one must describe forms of life, just as one must do to arrive at clarity on philosophical questions. However, the subsumption of an event under a causal law requires no such reaching down to a form of life.

What Wittgenstein said of mythical history also holds for history: 'One can only describe here, and say: "so it is in human life".'[26]

However, in order to be able to give the correct form of representation to a description, perspicuity is required as the ordering principle. In so far as this principle is primarily suited to that which possesses form (Gestalt), those who see a relationship between Wittgenstein and Gestalt psychology are at least aiming in the right direction, as has been contended by both myself and others elsewhere.[27] However, it was not Bühler who prompted Wittgenstein's line of thought, his turn towards a morphological (Goethean) way of thinking, but Spengler.

Notes

1. This is a revised version of a paper delivered in Budapest on 4 October 1980. An expanded version was read in Lisbon on 15 December of the same year. A Hungarian translation appeared in *Vilagossag* 5 (1981) under the title 'Wittgensteines Spengler'. I am indebted to B. McGuinness, M. Lourenco, Ch. Nyiri and A. Janik for their helpful remarks and clarifying suggestions. The present version was delivered at the 'Wittgenstein House' on Kundmanngasse in Vienna — now the Bulgarian Institute of Culture — on 29 August 1982.

2. Cf. Chapter 3.

3. Cf. Chapter 8.

4. O. Spengler, *The decline of the West, sketch of a morphology of the history of the world*, trans. C.F. Atkinson, (Knopf, New York, 1926). Originally published as *Der Untergang des Abendlandes, Gestalt und Wirklichkeit*, copyright 1918 by C.H. Beck, Munich. In the following, abbreviated as *Decline*.

5. A. Janik and S. Toulmin, *Wittgenstein's Vienna* (Simon and Schuster, New York, 1973).

6. Cf. O. Neurath, *Anti-Spengler* (1921), reprinted in R. Haller and H. Rutte (eds), *Gesammelte philosophische und methodologische Schriften*, vol. 1, (Hölder-Pichler-Tempsky, Vienna, 1981), pp. 139-96; L. Nelson, *Spuk. Einweihung in das Geheimnis der Wahrsagekunst Oswald Spenglers und sonnenklarer Beweis der Unwiderleglichkeit seiner Weissagungen, nebst Beitragen sur Physiognomik des Zeitgeistes. Eine Pfingstgabe für alle Adepten des metaphysischen Schauens* (1921), reprinted in Leonard Nelson, *Gesammelte Schriften*, vol. 3 (Meiner, Hamburg, 1974), pp. 349-552.

7. M. Schlick, *Aphorismen*, ed. B. Hardy Schlick, (Vienna, 1962), p. 39.

8. Ibid., p. 37; see also p. 17.

9. Cf. R. Haller, 'New light on the Vienna Circle', *Monist*, 65 (1982), pp. 25-37.

10. It is not surprising that Neurath, when speaking of the 'vast exaggerations' of certain influential authors, mentions Weininger and Spengler in the same breath. Cf. Neurath, *Anti-Spengler*, p. 147.

11. Spengler, *The decline of the West.*

12. Ibid.

13. Cf. Nelson, *Spuk*, pp. 391ff.

14. CV p. 74e.

15. Ibid., p. 37e.

16. Christian von Ehrenfels, *Kosmogonie* (Eugen Diederichs, Jena, 1916), p. 94.

17. BB p. 18.

18. See also R. Haller 'Philosophische Irrtümer und die Sprache' in E. Leinfellner, W. Leinfellner, H. Berghelt,and A. Hübner (eds) *Wittgenstein and his impact on contemporary thought* (Hölder-Pichler-Temsky, Vienna, 1978), pp. 298f; reprinted in R. Haller, *Studien zur Oesterreichischen Philosophie* (Rodopi, Amsterdam, 1979), ch. X.

19. PI I §568.

20. Ibid., I §66.

21. Ibid., I §654; cf. L. Wittgenstein, *Remarks on colour*, ed. E. Anscombe (Basil Blackwell, Oxford, 1977), III 230; L. Wittgenstein, 'Cause and effect: intuitive awareness', ed. R. Rhees, *Philosophia*, 6 (1976), p. 421.

22. CV p. 61e.

23. Ibid., p. 72e. At several points in his work, Wittgenstein uses the comparison of painting with describing, for purposes of clarification. He mentions sketches of the 'landscape of conceptual relations' (p. 78e), the 'details of an immense landscape' (p. 56e) that he shows to his students, and remarks that 'everything that comes my way becomes a picture' (p. 31e). Finally, he confesses: 'And after all a painter is basically what I am, often a very bad painter too' (p. 82e).

24. Cf. L. Wittgenstein, 'Remarks on Frazer's *Golden Bough*', ed. R. Rhees, trans. A.C. Miles, revsd R. Rhees (Brynmill Press, Retbid, 1979), p. 9e, where an earlier version of the passage occurring in the *Philosophical investigations*, I §122, can be found, containing Spengler's name!

25. PI I §126; cf. LA.

26. Wittgenstein, 'Remarks on Frazer's *Golden Bough*', p. 3e.

27. Cf. William Bartley III, 'Sprach- und Wissenschafttheorie als Werkzeuge einer Schulreform: Wittgenstein und Popper als oesterreichische Schullehrer, *Conceptus*, 3 (1969), pp. 6-22; and William Bartley III, *Wittgenstein* (J.B. Lippincott, Philadelphia-New York, 1973); as well as my review of Bartley, *Wittgenstein* in *Conceptus*, 11 (1977), pp. 422-4.

6

What do Wittgenstein and Weininger have in Common?

Only in recent years have people begun to ask why Wittgenstein found the work of Weininger worth mentioning (and indeed, worth recommending). It could not be said that the riddle of this strange connection has been clarified, much less solved in the few treatments that it has received in the philosophical literature.[1] What is the riddle, exactly? The most interesting puzzle is that concerning the possibility that Weininger influenced Wittgenstein philosophically. Thus, in the remarks that follow, I will not be concerned with similarities of general worldview or with attitudes on feminity or Jewishness, but rather solely with the question: what deeper philosophical common ground exists between the young and talented author of a provocative and widely-read book and the author of the *Tractatus* nine years his junior?

I will take as the starting point for my discussion the list of the authors whom Wittgenstein spoke of as having influenced him and as having provoked the beginnings of 'trains of thought'. As in the case of Wittgenstein and Spengler, I will ask what it could have been that motivated Wittgenstein to mention the name of Weininger, along with those of Boltzmann and Hertz on the one hand, and Frege and Russell on the other, as well as those of Karl Kraus, Adolf Loos and Oswald Spengler, as influential figures in his life. Briefly, what did Wittgenstein have in common with Weininger?

Previous answers to this question are based upon isolated similarities between the two thinkers. For example, Janik points out that Wittgenstein's moral conception of life approaches the 'ethical rigorism' of Weininger. Janik sees in Weininger's ethical theory 'a strict interpretation of Kant's categorical imperative. The moral man is the man who acts for the sake of duty alone.'[2]

Only in this connection (and in only half a paragraph) does Janik touch on what essentially connects the two thinkers: the close relation, a relation close to equation, that they find between logic and ethics.[3] Neither Lucka, nor Janik, who willingly follows Lucka, nor any other recent interpreter of Wittgenstein gives this aspect of his character the attention it deserves. On the contrary, Wittgenstein's way of thinking is, in Janik's view for example, that of an existentialist thinker, who, like Karl Jaspers, is fundamentally concerned to interpret the border regions of human existence, and their ciphers, as a rationally unanalysable world that 'points' to the ethical.

> If Wittgenstein is a Weiningerian as I claim, ... he, like Jaspers and also Lukacs, Heidegger and Berdyaev to name but a few, is developing certain Kantian themes concerning the relation between subject and object, the primacy of the moral over the epistemological and the notion of totality which are characteristic of the Southwest German School.[4]

It is not my purpose to address the problem of Wittgenstein's conception of ethics in this essay. I believe that Janik, like McGuinness, Winch, and others before them, correctly note a certain pre-eminence of moral concerns in Wittgenstein's work. Clear evidence for this view is to be found not only in the famous passage from the correspondence with Ludwig von Ficker, but also in the entire structure of the *Tractatus*. The boundary between that region of which one can speak, and that region of which it is proper to keep silent is surely also the boundary between practical and theoretical reason. And the solutions to the problems of 'theoretical reason' are not solutions to moral questions — and thus, surely, no solutions to the problems of life.

Nothing shows more clearly the dualism of facts and values that marks Wittgenstein's ethics than the sentence: 'All of the facts belong only to the problem, not to its solution.'[5] It is the possibility of being described or portrayed that distinguishes, ontologically and epistemologically, between that about which something *can be said* and that about which *nothing can be said.* The ethical, however, belongs entirely to that realm about which it is only proper to keep silence: 'It is clear that ethics cannot be put into words' (TLP 6.421). Wittgenstein derives this claim on the one hand from his judgement of facts: facts are not carriers of values; even their totality has no meaning. On the other hand —

and this is the other premiss — facts are always merely relative and accidental, while values are absolute and necessary. Because the sense of propositions can only be expressed through facts, inasmuch as every sentence sign that is used as an expression is itself a fact, that which goes beyond facts cannot be expressed. Necessarily, it cannot be said.

There is little to be said for the view that this conception of ethics has something in common with Kant's ethic of duty (as Janik's interpretation suggests). Even if the categorical imperative is regarded as a formal rule with a claim to universality, its application presupposes the rational device of distinguishing means from ends, and ends from ends-in-themselves, while Wittgenstein's argument is based on the belief that values exist. It is said of these values, moreover, that they lie 'outside the world'; and, second, that they cannot be expressed or depicted in meaningful language. Thus, the formulation of the categorical imperative must be senseless, taken as a fundamental moral principle, since, according to Wittgenstein, there can be 'no propositions of ethics' (TLP 6.62). If someone nevertheless formulates and asserts such a proposition, then that which is spoken has no meaning. Such a view should not be mentioned in the same breath as Kant's view, since it is in fact its polar opposite. While in the *Critique of practical reason*, Kant is concerned not with the knowledge of objects but with the capacity to make something real (by means of the will, a causality of a higher order), Wittgenstein, in contrast, clearly denies the existence of just this capacity. 'It is impossible to speak about the will in so far as it is the subject of ethical attributes.'[6] The will does not produce moral events, if it produces events at all. For the 'good will' and the 'evil will' do not change the facts; they leave everything as it is. When Wittgenstein insists that the world, independent of will, and thus also, of my will (TLP 6.373) is, as it is, — this is a clear consequence of his fundamental thesis, that only logical modalities and for that reason only logical necessity exists. For this reason, there is for Wittgenstein neither causal necessity nor a *causa noumenon* — a causality of freedom.[7]

In those passages where Weininger presents his ethical theory, he appears to hold a Kantian position. However, the main source of his metaphysics of the position of the ego and of sexual polarity is to be found in Schopenhauer. Like Kant, Weininger takes man's intellectual being as his true being, to which the empirical ego is and remains obligated. But Weininger identifies not only a categorical imperative, in which the moral law manifests itself, but also a logical imperative, in accordance with which logical rules are shown to be norms. And both imperatives require, in the last instance, that virtue and holiness, insight and wisdom are obligations to oneself. Although the metaphysical argument contributes nothing that is completely novel, they contain essential elements that go beyond Schopenhauer.

Weininger's originality is to be seen in the way that he follows ideas through to their ultimate consequences: the idea of the bisexuality of living beings, of the character of the feminine, as well as the idea of solipsism. However, this young intellectual from Vienna surely did not depend on either Schopenhauer or Kant in his metaphysics of logic, if one understands by this the fundamental thesis of the *unity of logic and ethics*. In fact, this idea of unity is at the heart of Weininger's metaphysics; it provides the missing link between the philosophy of the *Tractatus* and Weininger's theory of sexuality.[8]

I claimed earlier that Wittgenstein subordinates scientific and epistemological questions to moral behaviour. Like Kant, he countenances the primacy of practical reason. But the justification for this primacy is unavailable, since Wittgenstein did not (and could not) develop his ethics. Already in the preface to the *Tractatus*, Wittgenstein had claimed that little would be accomplished even by the solution of philosophical and scientific problems, and that the problems of life would remain untouched. Ethics, as Wittgenstein understands it, is not one of the sciences; 'in no sense do ethical judgements add anything to our knowledge'.[9] And, as we know from the *Tractatus*, the same is true of aesthetic judgements: 'Ethics and aesthetics are one' — both are, in Wittgenstein's usage, 'transcendental'. The decisive point in Wittgenstein's teaching is thus to characterise ethics and aesthetics in just the same way as logic, since from proposition 6.13 in the *Tractatus*, it is also true that 'Logic is transcendental.'[10] It is clear, then, that what logical and ethical propositions have in common is that neither can be confirmed or refuted by any possible experience (TLP 6.1112). They are beyond judgements of fact. However, logical and ethical propositions have a connection to the world that goes beyond the obtaining or non-obtaining of states of affairs: logical sentences present the skeletal structure of the world; ethical sentences express absolute values. Since, according to the linguistic rules of the *Tractatus*, only judgements of fact are expressible and meaningful propositions, logical propositions are, like ethical propositions, meaningless pointing-propositions. They point at something, but it is impossible to say in what the relationship of pointing consists, or even that such a relationship exists — when speaking of the relationship between language and world or that between willing and the good. Every attempt to articulate this in language is like vainly flying into the bars of a cage. Admittedly, the cage image comes from a later period in Wittgenstein's thought, while the foundation of his ethics took shape very early and did not change in any fundamental way in his later development.

It was clear from the beginning that Wittgenstein's doctrine of happiness has nothing to do with ordinary eudaimonism. He is certain only that the world of the happy person is a different world from the world of the unhappy person.[11] One day after the 27-year-old Wittgenstein noted this discovery, he asked himself — in the entry dated 30 July 1916 in his journal — how the imperative 'Be happy!' could be justified. His answer is fundamentalistic; he says, 'it appears that the happy life itself establishes that it is the only proper life'. That means either that there is no justification or that the justification is to be found in the meaning of being happy. There is every reason to believe that Wittgenstein meant the latter. The happiness that is in question here is not the happiness of pleasure, of luxury, but rather a striving happiness, the 'life of knowledge (the examined life)'.[12] And it is just this life of knowledge that bestows the good conscience required by Christianity, in particular. Bernard Bolzano had said: 'To be happy and to make happy, that is the fate of man.' Wittgenstein accepts only the first half of the maxim, since, for Wittgenstein, ethics does not depend on the existence of any being other than the moral subject, that is, of any being other than oneself.

At this point, another theme of Weininger's becomes relevant: the theme of solipsism:

> The human being is alone in the cosmos, in eternal, terrible loneliness. He has no purpose outside himself, nothing outside of himself for which he lives — he has flown far from wanting to be a slave, being able to be a slave, having to be a slave: all human society recedes under him. Social ethics recedes; he is alone, *alone*.[13]

This loneliness is not presented as an existential state but as an ontological given. In human beings, and in significant or noteworthy human beings in particular, the cosmos is not just reflected — 'the whole world' *is* in such a human being. In the great artist, the real genius, the world and the I *become one*: 'The great philosopher like the great artist possesses the whole world in himself; they are the conscious microcosms', reads one of Weininger's last writings.[14] The claim that the ego and the world are one — the soul of the human being *is* the microcosm — is used to make plausible the idea that, since the whole world is living in the soul of the human being, men can 'become women'. Since, according to Weininger, only men can become geniuses, can have soul, individuality, or an intelligible I, only men can become one with the world, or form true judgements of the world: 'The faculty of judgement — presupposing what lies in the most general way at its base, the presupposition that the human being is capable of judging everything — is only the dry, logical expression of the theory that the soul of the human being is a microcosm.'[15] The *Tractatus* echoes this thought: 'I am my world. (The Microcosm.)' (TLP 5.63). The following proposition precedes this famous passage in the *Tractatus*:

> For what the solipsist *means* is quite correct; only it cannot be *said*, but makes itself manifest. The world is *my* world: this is manifest in the fact that the limits of *language* (of that language which alone I understand) mean the limits of *my* world. (TLP 5.62)

One could easily dispute whether the passages discussed in the last couple of paragraphs were not inspired by Schopenhauer rather than by Weininger. Hacker does not even consider the possibility that the thesis 'that the human being is the microcosm, that I am the world' could originate with anyone other than Schopenhauer. It is simply a given, for Hacker, that 'Wittgenstein's solipsism was inspired by Schopenhauer's doctrine of transcendental idealism', and he calls this form of solipsism 'transcendental'. One cannot deny that Hacker alludes to a text of which Wittgenstein was aware. However, Hacker does not fully investigate the origin of this thought. Otherwise, it would have occurred to him that the source for the connection between logic and ethics is not obviously the same as the source for the form of the solipsistic thought in *The world as will and idea*.[16]

There is, in fact, little to be said for the claim that the idea of the I as microcosm and as solipsistic isolation — with all its attendant unclarities — is derived from reading Schopenhauer.[17] And surely no one could have found the close connection between logic and ethics asserted *there*. This thought is a typical product of the Weiningerian metaphysics; the author of *Sex and character* was well aware of the independence of this metaphysics when he said that he had to 'produce for himself'[18] not only the psychological–philosophical foundation of his doctrine, but also its logical–ethical foundation. But, as we have already seen, hardly any of Wittgenstein's interpreters have even referred to Weininger, and almost no one has recognised the respects in which Wittgenstein and Weininger agree. For surely they do *not* agree on the essential questions; for example, the question of what philosophy is, although even here there are affinities and points of contact between their views. Such a claim is only acceptable if one sees in Wittgenstein not the founder of the new Viennese positivism but of a philosophical dualism between that which can be grasped by knowledge (the sayable) and that which cannot be grasped by knowledge (the mystical): a dualism in which only the one domain, the 'worldly domain', if I may say so, seeks a logical, language-critical transparency, while the other is hidden by a commandment of silence: 'Everything that can be thought at all can be thought clearly. Everything that can be put into words can be put clearly'[19] '... and what we cannot talk about we must pass over in silence.'[20] The definition of all philosophising is derived from the professed intention to set a limit upon thinking and language: logical clarification of thought — briefly, critique of language. In contrast, for Weininger, those who set this task for philosophy were primarily 'flatheads'.[21] Otto Neurath always opposed just this dualism in Wittgenstein's thought, as a 'dual language idealism' (*doppelsprachige Idealistik*) and as metaphysics. And one must admit that the characterisation is accurate. There are two ways in which we are affected by signs: the one way directs itself to our understanding, with the Cartesian requirement of clearness and distinctness. The other directs itself to our intelligible I, as Weininger said, and as Wittgenstein could no longer say. For the consequence that he wants us to acknowledge is one of a most extreme rigour: keeping silence is the only command; but our 'keeping silent', as Wittgenstein expresses the command and as Neurath mocks it, is always keeping silent *about* something.

As Wittgenstein came to see the connection between logic and ethics, he also arrived at the perspective from which logic, ethics, and aesthetics see and comprehend the world. This is the perspective of which he writes in the journals — it sees objects not from their centre but 'from outside': 'So that they have the whole world as background.'[22] From this point, he takes up Weininger's reflection on whether the spirit that is my spirit is the same spirit as the spirit of the world. Just this obscure idea — a clear consequence of the notion of a microcosm — connects Wittgenstein with his solipsistic metaphysics:

> This is the way that I have travelled: Idealism singles men out from the world as unique, solipsism singles me alone out, and at last I see that I too belong with the rest of the world, and so on the one side *nothing* is left over, and on the other side, as unique, *the world.* In their way idealism leads to realism if it is strictly thought out.

What follows in the *Tractatus* is the well-known passage which is supposed to show that one can legitimately speak in philosophy of an I in a non-psychological sense, that is, as metaphysical subject, the limit of the world: 'What brings the self into philosophy is the fact that "the world is my world"' (TLP 5.641).

However, the outside perspective is also the starting point for the connection between logic and ethics. Just as ethical propositions do not express what it is to be happy, so logical propositions do not express what is mirrored in them. We have one and the same sign for the identity of one and the same object, and that it is the same is expressed by its form. But we experience that it does mean the same either through use or through the rules that guide it. At this point we encounter the deepest basis for the common ground between Weininger and Wittgenstein: both believe that neither logical nor ethical rules can be established, but yet that both logical and ethical rules have an essential connection to the world and are thus one and the same. For Wittgenstein, all the great questions of metaphysics lead into this connection — questions to which the only appropriate answer is silence, since the questions cannot be answered within the world — that is, clearly and precisely.

Notes

1. Cf. Allan Janik, 'Wittgenstein and Weininger', in: *Akten des 2. Int. Wittgenstein Symposiums 29.8-4.9, 1977*, (Hölder-Pichler Tempsky, Vienna, 1978), reprinted in A. Janik, *Essays on Wittgenstein and Weininger* (Studien zur Östereichischen Philosophie IX), (Rodopi, Amsterdam, 1985), pp. 64-72; K. Mulligan, 'Philosophy, animality and justice: Kleist, Kafka, Weininger, and Wittgenstein', in B. Smith (ed.), *Structure and Gestalt: philosophy and literature in Austria-Hungary and her successor states* (Linguistic and Literary Studies in Eastern Europe), (John Benjamins B.V., Amsterdam, 1981); B. Smith, 'Weininger and Wittgenstein', in B.F. McGuinness and A. Gargani, (eds), *Wittgenstein and contemporary philosophy Teoria*, V (1985), pp. 227-57; Jacques LeRider, *Der Fall Otto Weininger. Wurzeln des Antifeminismus und Anti-semitismus* (Löcker, Vienna, 1985). See also R. Haller, *Fragen zu Wittgenstein und Aufsätze zur Österreichischen Philosophie* (Studien zur Österreichischen Philosophie X), (Rodopi, Amsterdam, 1986), p. 176.

2. Janik, *Essays on Wittgenstein and Weininger*, p. 71.

3. Ibid., pp. 71, 85.

4. Allan Janik, 'Philosophical sources on Wittgenstein's ethics', in Janik, *Essays on Wittgenstein and Weininger*, p. 94.

5. TLP 6.4321.

6. TLP 6.423. Cf. NB 'I want to call the "will" primarily the bearer of good and evil.' (Entry for 21 July 1916.)

7. Cf. I. Kant, *Critique of practical reason* (German: Akademie Ausgabe), vol. V, pp. 55, 94, 105, 114.

8. Cf. O. Weininger, *Über die letzten Dinge* ('On Things') (Vienna-Leipzig, 1918). See also LeRider, *Der Fall Otto Weininger. Wurzeln des Antifeminismus und Anti-semitismus*; and J. LeRider and N. Leser (eds), *Otto Weininger. Werk und Wirkung* (Quellen und Studien zur Oesterreichischen Geistesgeschichte im 19. und 20. Jahrhundert, vol. 5) (Oesterr. Bundesverlag, Vienna, 1984).

9. L. Wittgenstein, *Lecture on ethics*.

10. That the term 'transcendental' is not meant in the Kantian sense here is apparent, though apparently not to all interpreters. See Chapter 3; also S. Thiele, *Die Verwicklungen im Denken Wittgenstein* (Alber, Freiburg, 1983), p. 63. In fact, the first statement concerning the transcendental character of ethics applies the term 'transcendent' and not the term 'transcendental'. Cf. NB entry for 30 July 1916. Not very convincing on this passage is F. Wallner, *Die Grenzen der Sprache und der Erkenntnis* (*Philosophica* 1), (Braumüller, Vienna, 1983), pp. 160f. Naturally, the 'horizon' (*Grenze*), as he says, is not a rule of measure for correct judgements, just as the statements of logic are not 'abstractions from meaningful statements', and statements of ethics are not 'abstractions from actions'.

11. TLP 6.43: 'The world of the happy man is a different one from that of the unhappy man.' Cf. NB entry for 29 July 1916. See also R. Haller, 'Philosophieren — Arbeit an einem selbst?' in P. Kruntorad (ed.), *A.E.I.O.U.* (Österr. Bundesverlag, Vienna, 1985), pp. 70ff. Two years before these notes were written, Wittgenstein 'bought and read' vol. 8 of Nietzche's works (containing *The twilight of the gods, Antichrist* and *Ecce*

homo), writing in the so-called 'Secret notebook', 8 December 1914; 'Am however moved by his animosity towards Christianity. For there is some truth in his writings. Surely, that Christianity is the only *sure* way to happiness. But what if one scorns this happiness? Could it not be better to be unhappy, to come to ruin in hopeless conflict with the external world? But such a life is senseless. But why not lead a senseless life? Is it unworthy? How is it to be reconciled with the solipsistic standpoint? What must I do then, that I do not lose my life? I must have before me always an awareness of the Spirit.' In L. Wittgenstein, 'Geheime Tagebucher: Der verschlüsselte Teil der "Gmundener Notizbücher",' ed. W. Baum, *Saber*, vol. 6 (1985), pp. 475f.

12. NB entry for 13 August 1916.

13. Otto Weininger, *Geschlecht und Charakter* ('Sex and Character'), p. 203, cf. p. 234.

14. Weininger, *Über die letzten Dinge*, p. 169.

15. Ibid., p. 246.

16. Cf. P.M.S. Hacker, *Insight and illusion* (Oxford University Press, Oxford, 1972), p. 2.

17. Cf. NB entry for 2 August 1916: 'One could say (with Schopenhauer): The world of ideas is neither good nor evil, but is rather the subject that wills.'

18. Weininger, *Über die letzten Dinge*, p. viii.

19. TLP 4.116.

20. Ibid., Foreword.

21. O. Weininger, 'From Bacon to Fritz Mauthner, all lowbrows have been *critics of language*', *Über die letzten Dinge*, p. 171.

22. NB entry for 7 October 1916.

23. L.W. Wittgenstein, *Notebooks 1914-1916*, G.H. von Wright and G.E.M. Anscombe eds (Oxford: Basil Blackwell, 1961), p. 85e, G.E.M. Anscombe, trans.

7

Was Wittgenstein a Sceptic?
or
On the Differences Between Two 'Battle Cries'

This is a curious question, and it may also seem to be a misguided one, to anyone who 'knows' that Wittgenstein was not a sceptic. If one asks a misplaced and inappropriate question, one ought not be surprised at receiving a misplaced and inappropriate answer, if one receives an answer at all. Should one fail to find an answer, then it would be suitable to ask oneself why this question had been posed at all, if it was to be left unanswered.

A philosophical education, or even general intellectual acumen, would counsel us that whoever makes the claim that there are physical objects advances a *philosophical* thesis and not a physical one. Presumably, such an assertion as 'There are physical objects' is directed against the negation of the assertion of the existence of physical objects. And whoever says 'There are no physical objects' likewise makes something that we must regard as a philosophical claim.

If the person who asserts the existence of physical objects (whatever it may be that he is thereby asserting) can be called a *realist*, where being a realist entails, for instance, alleging that one is able to demonstrate the existence of a *res extensa* that is independent of a *res cogitans* or an ego, then we may well call any philosopher who rejects this argument and the realist's thesis an idealist — provided that he claims physical objects are dependent upon an ego, upon thought, or the like.

It could be said of the latter's position that it is sceptical with regard to his opponent's (the realist's) position, and this accords with the customary usage of the term 'sceptical'. Hence, whoever denies our everyday belief in the existence of physical objects, is sceptical with regard to this one particular postulation, and Wittgenstein calls this view the 'idealist's scepticism'.[1]

Thus one who doubts that there exist physical objects, or that the object which I take to be my hand *is* in fact my hand, is — since he doubts this — a sceptic, but he is a sceptic only with respect to the positive assertion (that the object is in fact my hand). He may hold the belief that there are no physical objects and that what we take to be physical objects are actually something quite different, say, sensations or representations. That is to say, the negative assertions and the positive ones are *on the same level*. Just as Carnap, in *Pseudoproblems in philosophy*, first raises the question of 'whether the theses mentioned here have any scientific sense at all',[2] Wittgenstein begins likewise by saying that the proposition 'There are physical objects' is 'nonsense', by denying even the possibility of formulating this proposition.[3]

This is, of course, no superficial scepticism about a positive assertion, but a more thoroughgoing one, which calls into question the legitimacy of *both* kinds of assertion. And calling 'legitimacy' into question here signifies nothing more than the assertion that no truth-value can be attributed to a nonsensical proposition.

Were one to wonder why the proposition should be nonsensical, the following suggests itself as a reply: If the proposition 'There are physical objects' does have sense, then it would, presumably, have to be an empirical proposition, a proposition about experience. But what kind of experience could it be about; by what kind of experience could it or its negation be confirmed? The answer is that there is no experience that would satisfy such a proposition; it is a pseudo-proposition which does not actually touch upon experience, but rather goes beyond it.

However — as Wittgenstein rejoins to his own line of reasoning — does being informed that this kind of proposition is nonsensical suffice to convince either the idealist or the realist that it is nonsense to assert something like this? Evidently not. Of course, neither does it suffice to support the dogmatic defence of common sense.

When we claim to know something, then it is necessary for the truth of this claim not only that we are convinced of it and have sufficient reasons for believing it, but also that it is true. If, however, we cannot convince ourselves of its truth other than by giving justifications for the reasons which we have to support the claim to its truth, then how can we sustain the claim to knowledge? Is there not more at issue here than just *one* chain of justifications for *one* assertion? And aren't the very foundations of our empirical judgements at stake here? That someone believes that he knows something does just as little to justify his assertion as his assurances and reaffirmations do, that he does indeed know such-and-such to be the case (cf. OC §137).

Wittgenstein seems quite clearly to believe that it is not *one* assertion that is questioned or defended in the case of an epistemic doubt. When we are learning the role of empirical judgements, we do not simply learn *rules*, but a 'totality of judgements is made plausible to us' (OC §140):

> When we first begin to *believe* anything, what we believe is not a simple proposition, it is a whole system of propositions. (OC §141)

> It is not single axioms that strike me as obvious, it is a system in which consequences and premises give one another mutual support. (OC §142)

Wittgenstein advances the view, in several passages throughout his writings that a whole system of propositions is involved with our beliefs. And I regard this view as fundamental for what may be called a paradigm in Thomas Kuhn's sense, since — although I shall not enter into this here — it is fundamental to the general sort of justification given for 'worldviews'. For example, consider our belief that the world is round, a belief that has continued to receive confirmation, beginning with the exploratory voyages of the fifteen century, from Amerigo Vespucci to the age of artificial satellites:

> We know that the earth is round. We have definitively ascertained that it is round. We shall stick to this opinion ... (OC §291)

> Further experiments cannot *give the lie* to our earlier ones, at most they may change our whole way of looking at things. (OC § 292)

The truth alluded to here, then, seems just as definitive as the truth of the propositions in the *Tractatus*: 'We shall stick to this opinion.' Can doubts be raised here, such as those that were raised, for example, by Popper about a criterion of meaning — with an ironical nod to the author of the *Tractatus*?[4] Already before Popper's sarcasm, Wittgenstein had tried to show in his 'Big typescript' that suspicions of meaninglessness must not be raised dogmatically. That is to say, if we, for example, doubt whether the body that we are seeing is a sphere, we can very well hypothesise that it is not a sphere. It is one thing to be convinced that something has a spherical form, but it is something quite different to claim that something has such a form. For it is possible that the latter claim means that something *appears* to have such a form, and to cast *this* appearance in doubt, Wittgenstein argues, would suspend the function of the hypothesis:

> The mechanism of the hypothesis wouldn't function if the appearance were also questionable; if, that is, there were not a facet of the hypothesis that could be given indubitable verification.[5]

Fifteen years later, Wittgenstein writes: '... whenever we test anything, we are already presupposing something that is not tested' (OC §163). Wittgenstein clearly distinguishes between what is not verified but taken as an assumption or, occasionally, learned, and individual hypotheses. He calls the former the 'self-evident foundation' of research, such as that of, say, Lavoisier's research — a 'Weltbild' (cf. OC §167).

It seems to be Wittgenstein's conviction that only on the basis of such a worldview can true or false judgements be made and put to the test; that the question of the truth or falsity of statements which express the foundation of the worldview does not arise. One gradually becomes accustomed to a worldview; worldviews are adopted, believed in. But when the question 'Does my belief correspond to reality?' is raised, one finds out that no provisions have been made for *such* questions (cf. OC §318, §341). However, does this mean that what is not tested and also not doubted *cannot* be doubted? Not at all. Given only that we accept the principle of bivalence and that we can talk of doubting only where there is also the possibility of not doubting (OC §3), it does not follow that it is logically impossible to doubt any given proposition that is assumed to be true. Admittedly, we cannot doubt *everything*, since the indefinite expression 'everything' includes also the meanings or uses of the expressions in the language.[6]

> The *point* of the word 'all' is that it admits no exception. — True, that is the point of its use in our language; but the

kinds of use we feel to be the 'point' are connected with the role that such-and-such a use has in our whole life.[7]

Even if someone were to be, or become, convinced by the sceptical maxim that 'one cannot know anything', it would depend upon the particular activities that are closely bound to the language whether what he claimed *can* be said, in that indefinite sense of 'can' which may be called the 'logical can'. It is, nevertheless, by no means obvious what Wittgenstein actually means when he says that what counts as 'an adequate test' of a hypothesis belongs to logic. This claim is illuminated to an extent in his remark that 'it belongs to the description of the language game' (OC §82). Apparently, the following assertion also belongs to the description of the language game:

> In certain circumstances, a man cannot make a *mistake.*
> ('Can' is here used logically, and the proposition does not
> mean that a man cannot say anything false in those circum-
> stances.) If Moore were to pronounce the opposite of those
> propositions which he declares certain, we should not just
> share his opinion: we should regard him as demented. (OC
> §155)

> In order to make a mistake, a man must already judge
> in conformity with mankind. (OC §156)

As is often the case, Wittgenstein's reflections begin with an attempt to find a context for the use of the expressions that are under investigation, and he gives a number of examples the contexts for which do not permit the judgement that one is mistaken, e.g. '12 × 12 = 144', 'I have just had lunch', 'I have never been on the moon.' These examples show that if there are mistakes, there have to be different kinds of mistakes, and Wittgenstein does not exclude only mathematical judgements, i.e. judgements *a priori*, from the set of things about which one can be mistaken. However, towards the conclusion of his notes on certainty, Wittgenstein concedes that he is not able to give a 'general characterisation' of the cases in which someone may justifiably claim to be immune from error. It is therefore evident that no distinction can be drawn between cases where one is *nearly* immune from error and those in which one *cannot* be mistaken (OC §673, §674).

What, then, does the claim to immunity from error really mean? I think that we ought to keep two considerations separate in responding to this question: first, the question of the meaning of an assertion; and secondly, the question of the role of immunity from error in our actions or in our use of the language.[8]

It is not easy to determine which of the two questions is the more difficult one. To know what immunity from error means, we must know what an error is. And here it may occur to us that in the cases nearest at hand, we talk about an error when someone, although aware of what the correct choice would be, does something that is not right or says something that is not right or true. If we disregard most of the variety of ways in which we humans can err, and focus on the narrower range of *epistemic* concepts, then we can take 'error' to mean that the subject assumes, believes or claims to believe the existence of a state of affairs, and that the assertion of its existence does not hold true. This is what Wittgenstein means when he writes: 'And error belongs only with opinion.'[9] The proponent of an assertion which turns out to be false, although he is convinced of its truth, is mistaken. But in fact, we would not characterise all of the cases which fall under this description as errors! We do not in all cases *grant* someone the possibility that he *can* be mistaken. In so far as this is true. Wittgenstein is right in saying that 'the possibility of a *mistake* can be eliminated in certain (numerous) cases' (OC §650). But he is also right in assuming that we judge certain cases differently which, on grounds of definition or meaning would be characterised as errors, but for which 'no place is prepared in the game' (OC §647). These are, namely, those cases in which we do not accuse someone of a mistake who does or says something radically incorrect, something that neither he nor any fellow member of his community could seriously say, let alone hold for warranted, but rather regard the agent or speaker as *mentally defective*. If a man approached us and with complete earnestness stated repeatedly that he had — literally, not metaphorically — lost his head, our response would perhaps be to attempt to calm him, telling him 'you're mistaken, you still have your head'; if not, then we would not be of the opinion that he was mistaken, but rather that he is insane.

> Moore's mistake lies in this — countering the assertion that one cannot know that, by saying 'I do know it'. (OC §521)[10]

105

This is a mistake, solely for the reason that the claim to know is not sufficient to establish the truth of the claim to know: 'It is always by favour of Nature that one knows something' (OC §505). For

> Whether I *know* something depends on whether the evidence backs me up or contradicts me. (OC §504)

Whether the evidence actually backs up my claim does *not*, however, depend on *myself*, but on what is the case. And concerning the evidence itself, Wittgenstein very clearly advocates a form of the justificational model of knowledge, according to which every justification for an assertion or claim to know must, first, be finite, and, second, actually come to an end. The account presented by Wittgenstein differs from those accounts that attempt to locate the justification for a 'stopping-place' in self-presentations such as, for example, Meinong's and Chisholm's. The latter accounts must identify some sort of evidence of all evidence, whereas Wittgenstein needs only to point out that any given substantiation or justification actually *has* an end. In the *Brown book*, we read:

> And the mistake which we here and in a thousand similar cases are inclined to make is labelled by the word 'to make' as we have used it in the sentence 'It is no act of insight which makes us use the rules as we do', because there is an idea that 'something must make us' do as we do. And this again joins the confusion between cause and reason. *We have no reason to follow the rules as we do.* The chain of reasons has an end.[11]

In this statement, a reply is provided to the second question, which has, so far, been neglected: i.e. the question of the part played by immunity from error in our actions and in our language games. For the present, we have to establish that the method of doubt is the method for ascertaining immunity from error, and it is almost beyond question that Wittgenstein takes a non-Cartesian stance here, as Anthony Kenny has already pointed out:[12]

> It belongs to the logic of our scientific investigations that certain things are *in deed* not doubted. (OC §342)

... that absence of doubt belongs to the essence of the language game ... (OC §370)

If you tried to doubt everything you would not get as far as doubting anything. The game of doubting itself presupposes certainty. (OC §115)

Even if the method of doubt may be called Cartesian, its *application* nevertheless shows that it is not the Cartesian method that is involved here. First of all, as we have seen, doubt is restricted: one who doubts everything would also have to doubt the meanings of the expressions in his language. But then he could not possibly know what it was he was doing when doubting everything. Secondly, in the case of doubt we presuppose that it may be *shown* what speaks for or against an assumption (cf. OC §117). That is to say, there is need here as well for accepted criteria, and I cannot call into question the validity of all of these criteria at once, since I need at least some of them to apply as criteria. (When I doubt whether the kilogram of bread that I am buying actually weighs a kilogram I cannot, when testing my supposition, simultaneously doubt that the weight used to correspond to a standard kilogram *and* doubt the test that would decide the first question.) Thirdly, when forming judgements on something, we do not judge against the background of a *tabula rasa*, but against the background of a world-picture that incorporates not only a set of true sentences which we believe or take as assumptions, — that is, not only that of which we are convinced, — but also a great deal that we accept unquestioningly, and on the basis of which we test and verify hypotheses, distribute truth-values, and even attempt to convince others to give up their conceptual framework.

If we accept the broad use that Wittgenstein made of the notion of a language game, what we have said thus far will also apply to language games. Just as 'the *truth* of so certain empirical propositions belongs to our frame of reference' (OC §83) so certain assumptions and epistemic attitudes (believing, holding true, knowing) belong likewise to the basis of thinking and acting. Von Wright has aptly called this basis a 'pre-knowledge'. Such knowledge is in its very essence not propositional, but practical knowledge, a 'know-how', which, however, unlike most 'know-how', cannot be traced back to or reduced to a 'knowledge-that'.

Although Wittgenstein thus rejects a reductionist programme,

the justification of knowledge does not thereby lose its foundation. On the contrary: it gains a new one, whose explication is,
admittedly, not given, though this does not mean that it could
not be given.[13]

If Wittgenstein's analysis — in so far as it is an analysis —
shows clear signs of deviating from programmes of the Cartesian
nature, it nevertheless remains within that programme to a
certain extent. I mean by this that although there may be a
number of indications that Wittgenstein abandoned the search
for foundations, his own non-reductionist foundation for the
justificational theory of knowledge shows that this is not so. This
is not to deny that he frequently pointed out the proximity of the
concept of knowledge to that of *decision*, or that he applied the
idea of a *construction* to replace the 'chain of reasons', but as it
seems to me at least, he leaves no doubt *in the crucial passages* that,
firstly, our claims to knowledge are justified by reasons; secondly,
the chain of reasons or justification for what we know has a *finite
end*; and, thirdly, that the totality of what we know has foundations. Since these foundations must be on a *different level* from
the judgements they sustain, we might suspect that Wittgenstein
was attracted to the non-foundationalist conception of knowledge, as if Wittgenstein were a precursor of Sir Karl Popper or
Paul Feyerabend! To an extent, then, he does remain within the
framework of the Cartesian programme, and as everyone knows,
this programme is primarily characterised by the possibility of
doubt about all instances of possible knowledge. As Schlick has
pointed out:

> All important attempts at establishing a theory of know-
> ledge grow out of the problem concerning the *certainty* of
> human knowledge. And this problem in turn originates in
> the wish for absolute certainty.[14]

However, the methods that Wittgenstein proposes and applies,
though intended for mere description, do not seem to admit the
possibility of *absolute certainty*. But Wittgenstein also has a method
for establishing, and perhaps, for producing, unshakeable
certainty — and this, I suppose, means absolute certainty:

> To accept a proposition as unshakeably certain — I want to
> say — means to use it as a grammatical rule: this removes
> uncertainty from it.[15]

To put it a bit differently, by using a sentence as a grammatical rule, we acknowledge its unassailable certainty. At times, it appears as though such sentences are supposed to provide foundations that lie *within* the language game; a basis, as it were, beneath which one cannot venture. At other times, it appears as if what is excluded from the uncertain is made certain in virtue of being used as a *norm* for what is certain. And this theme recurs frequently in Wittgenstein: that a well-confirmed empirical proposition may also be used as a norm (or criterion).[16] But even were one to prefer the latter interpretation, the former is not yet invalidated, since both is in agreement to the extent that they concern actions which give meaning to linguistic expressions through their use. The justification for such a ground is neither possible nor meaningful unless one resorts to the commonplace that one's life just is as it is, and that we can go no further, in any investigation, than our life itself. A claim such as the claim that the justification for this ultimate foundation is neither meaningful nor possible may also be understood as a claim about the limits of reason, which denies in principle the possibility of revealing the conditions of the foundation.

Wittgenstein's 'solution' of the problem of the foundation of knowledge — there is, indeed, not only *this* problem of foundations — thus contains a quasi-sceptical and a quasi-pragmatic component and the first is connected with the latter.

In *On Certainty* he writes:

> But I did not get my picture of the world by satisfying myself of its correctness; nor do I have it because I am satisfied of its correctness. No: it is the inherited background against which I distinguish between true and false. (OC §94)

From this it clearly follows that the worldview is not a network of convictions whose correctness are in need of testing. Rather, our worldview constitutes the background for our convictions, whose truth or falsity is in question and which must be put to the test. The correctness (truth or falsity) of the worldview itself, however, lies outside the scope of any such test.[17] In other words: if the 'background' has no propositional content, i.e. cannot be judged as to its truth or falsity, it becomes clear why it is that whoever is 'mistaken' with respect so it cannot be mistaken only in an ordinary sense, but must be regarded as completely foreign or even as demented. From this, there emerges a quasi-pragmatic cast to the problem of knowledge: proceeding from the supposition that it is not a state of affairs in itself which determines what we will and will not accept as an observation sentence, because those states of affairs are themselves conditioned by circumstances identified and interpreted by ourselves, then the manner of our thinking depends upon our own determinations. If, however, our determinations rest upon a non-propositional basis, then the distinction between truth and falsity cannot be applied to them; rather, the totality of agreements with that which we can refer to as our 'worldview' must serve as our criterion.

As is well known, not only by those who research the psychology of perception and observation but by many others, there are cases in which something might be *seen as*, or *observed as*, so-and-so. This kind of case was of central concern in Wittgenstein's philosophy of psychology. The same kind of case, however, appears in the study of the interpretation of texts as well, since what is meant by certain phrases might be 'seen' in different ways, depending upon how one looks at the text in question.

At least since Stanley Cavell pointed out the parallels between a 'grammatical' investigation in Wittgenstein's sense and a *transcendental* one in Kant's sense,[18] there have been attempts to apply Kantian philosophy as an interpretative framework for Wittgensein's *Philosophical investigations*. Since then, there have been a great many interpreters who have credited themselves with the discovery of a new Wittgenstein in the transcendental interpretation, and a new Kant in Wittgenstein's guise.

Some believe that Wittgenstein advocated, especially in the *Tractatus*, a position that would correspond to that of the *Critique of pure reason*, in determining the limits of possible experience. Others, again, believe that Wittgenstein's transition to his so-called 'later philosophy' also betrays a turn from a realist to a constructivist position. Some interpreters take the similarity between the two philosophers to consist in their entire approach; others, again, take it to consist in the ontological foundations, etc. Some of these interpretations have without any doubt yielded outstanding results, particularly those concerning the interpretation of Wittgenstein's philosophy of mathematics. Although these interpretations merit consideration, this is not the appropriate occasion for an investigation of the various results of this Gestalt-switch in the understanding of Wittgenstein. It must be admitted that an interpretation employing the refined conceptual framework of Kantian philosophy could elucidate some points that would probably not be brought to light were one to take other schemata as the basis of analysis. As important and interesting as this question may be, particularly in a period of neo-Kantianism, we must forego a discussion of it here.

Nevertheless we do have to occupy ourselves with no more than one small point from Kant, in the remainder of our argumentation. Returning to our initial question, the question of whether Wittgenstein was a sceptic — and at least his denial of the possibility of knowledge of oneself might give rise to such a suspicion — the Kantian characterisation of the sceptic and of scepticism seems to be helpful in providing a basis for judging the answer.

Kant draws a strict distinction between the *sceptical method* and *scepticism*. The former serves to provoke a controversy, 'not for the purpose of finally deciding in favour of either side, but to discover whether the object of the struggle is not a mere illusion'. 'This 'sceptical method' is oriented towards certainty in so far as it endeavours '... to detect the point of misunderstanding'.[19] In the sense in which grammatical investigations may be called transcendental, the method of 'discovering the point of misunderstanding' may be called sceptical. Indeed, we would have to refer to it in this way if we were to follow Kant, who regards this method as 'essentially peculiar to transcendental philosophy *only*'.[20]

In the 'Transcendental doctrine of method', in the section entitled 'The impossibility of a sceptical satisfaction of pure reason in its internal conflicts', an attempt is made to settle the question of whether a method that is designed to ascertain the limits of knowledge, is, or may be, called a dogmatic, a critical or a sceptical method. Here, the sceptic is described as the philosopher who, as a preliminary exercise, tests all of the assertions of uncritical dogmatism, rejects their unconditional validity and perhaps — like Hume — traces them back to habits. In a like manner, Wittgenstein occasionally 'reduces' the use of expressions to habit or to custom.

Whoever holds such a view may be called a sceptic in Kant's terms, regardless of whether he is ingenious or not. He does not get any further than 'subjecting the *facta* of reason to examination and eventually to disapproval'. In short, this is to appoint a censor of reason, and, thereby, to entertain 'doubt regarding all transcendental use of principles'. However, he will abstain from the last step, that of subjecting 'to examination ... reason itself, in the whole extent of its powers, and as regards its aptitude for pure *a priori* modes of knowledge', and thus to determine its 'definite limits', and will, at most, construct a 'resting place' for the orientation of reason, and not a 'dwelling-place for permanent domicile'.[21]

What the realist and the idealist *say*, whether it be a realism or idealism of the transcendental or of the empirical type, differs *in toto* not only from what they *do*, but also from the ground on which they play out their language game. Accordingly, if either one tries to teach a child the use of the expression 'chair', the differences will not be differences between the facts that are taught, nor will they be differences of languages used; they will rather, as Wittgenstein says, be differences between 'battle cries'.[22]

What moral may be drawn from this? There is, I believe, at least one important one, and I shall confine myself to it, for the present: before following Wittgenstein's suggestion that it is possible to 'see' any given philosopher in the light of many different philosophical interpretations, and before seeking resemblances between Wittgenstein and other philosophers, we should not forget to see what there is to see, and to try to pay attention to what Wittgenstein himself clearly recommended: to heed not the battle cries, but that which underlies them in the context of human action.

Notes

1. OC §37.
2. R. Carnap, *The logical structure of the world — pseudoproblems in philosophy*, trans. R.A. George (University of California Press, Berkeley, 1969), p. 61 (German edn, tr).
3. OC §35, §36.
4. K.R. Popper, *The logic of scientific discovery*, 2nd edn (Hutchinson, London, 1959), p. 22.
5. PG, pt I, p. 222.
6. Cf. ·R. Haller, 'Das cartesische Dilemma', *Zeitschrift für philosophische Forschung*, 18 (1964), pp. 369-85.
7. RFM I, 16; cf. I §§10ff.
8. Cf. R. Haller, 'Philosophische Irrtümer und die Sprache', in *Wittgenstein and his impact upon contemporary thought — proceedings of the 2nd international Wittgenstein symposium August 29-September 4 1977 Kirchberg/Wechsel*, eds E. Leinfellner *et al.*, (Hölder-Pichler-Tempsky,

Vienna, 1978), pp. 298-302.

9. L. Wittgenstein, 'Remarks on Frazer's *The Golden Bough*', ed. R. Rhees, trans. A.C. Miller, revsd R. Rees (Brynmill Press, Retford, 1979).

10. Cf. G.E. Moore 'A defence of common sense' in J.H. Muirhead (ed.), *Contemporary British philosophy*, 2nd series (London: 1924), pp. 193-223, repr. in G.E. Moore, *Philosophical Papers* (Routledge and Kegan Paul, London, 1959). Cf. also my review in *Philosophischer Literaturanzeiger*, 23 (1970), pp. 55-7.

11. BB, p. 143.

12. A. Kenny, *Wittgenstein*, (Harvard University Press, Cambridge, 1973), pp. 205ff.

13. Cf. R. Haller, 'Concerning the so-called Münchhausen trilemma', *Ratio*, 16 (1974), pp. 125-40.

14. M. Schlick, 'Über das Fundament der Erkenntnis', *Erkenntnis*, 4 (1934). English translation by D. Rynin, 'The foundation of knowledge', in A.J. Ayer (ed.), *Logical positivism* (The Free Press, New York, 1959), p. 209.

15. RFM II 39.

16. Recall the distinction between symptoms and criteria in, e.g. *Philosophical investigations*, I §34.

17. Cf. G.E.M. Anscombe, 'The question of linguistic idealism' (Essays on Wittgenstein in honor of G.H. von Wright), *Acta Philosophica Fennica*, vol. 28 (1976), pp. 209ff.

18. S. Cavell, 'The availability of Wittgenstein's later philosophy', *Philosophical Review*, 71 (1962), pp. 67-93.

19. I. Kant, *Critique of pure reason*, ed., trans N. Kemp Smith (St Martin's Press, New York, 1933) B 451f.

20. Ibid.

21. Ibid., B788-96.

22. Z §414.

8

The Common Behaviour of Mankind[1]

The problems concerning the presuppositions of utterances which are capable of being true or false, and the problems of their grounding and justification, are closely connected to one another. This connection is often overlooked. Whether a sentence of a language is true or false depends upon whether certain conditions are fulfilled which would allow the predication of a truth-value to it. Whether or not a sentence can be grounded depends upon whether or not it can be derived from other sentences, sentences which express grounds. And whether or not a person is justified in his epistemic attitudes depends on whether or not the chain of premisses supporting it is finite or infinite.

But not only logical relations belong to the grounding of a statement, and not only finite sets of premisses belong to epistemic justification. Moreover, it certainly is not the case that any descriptive statement has only one presupposition of some sort, which must be fulfilled if the statement is to be either true or false. In a broader sense, presuppositions, grounds, and justifications are themselves conditioned by the facts of nature and of history.

That such conditions play a significant role in Wittgenstein's philosophy has often been overlooked, because they don't lie on the surface. The conditions in question will elude discovery as long as one clings to the simple view that a bipartite Wittgenstein, a Wittgenstein I and a Wittgenstein II, is the key to interpreting his work.[2] I think it is the dominance of this interpretation that hindered recognition of the fact, that at least the aim of his philosophy suffered no great changes from the *Tractatus* to his last writings. It was always Wittgenstein's position, throughout the transformations undergone by his early point of view that philos-

114

ophy, as it is understood from the analytic point of view, has neither normative directives nor causal explanations among its results, but rather presumes that the results of philosophical labours inhere in the 'clarification of propositions'.³ 'For the clarity that we are aiming at is indeed *complete* clarity. But this simply means that the philosophical problems should *completely* disappear.'⁴ Since Wittgenstein never subordinated this aim to any other, the demand for clarity preserved its explosive power, inaugurating the philosophical turn that later came to be known as the linguistic turn.⁵

Although over a quarter of a century has passed since Wittgenstein's death, our understanding of his basic positions has acquired many perspectives, but few outlines which would be generally acknowledged. This becomes particularly obvious when we consider our understanding of the basic concepts and *leitmotivs* of Wittgenstein's philosophy.

The topic of the present discussion appears not to advert to such a basic topic, counter to what one would expect in a treatment of Wittgenstein's philosophy. And yet not only the description and the philosophy of language rests upon the ground with which this topic is concerned; but the fundamental *leitmotiv* of Wittgenstein's philosophy, the relation between language and reality, emerges on this ground, returning to it ever again.

What role, then, does the 'common behaviour of mankind' play in Wittgenstein's epistemology and philosophy of language? How can the fact that human beings act in similar ways under certain conditions and in particular situations be attributed with the significance that was accorded to the *sentence form* in the *Tractatus logico-philosophicus*? How would the 'common behaviour of mankind' serve as a *frame of reference* 'by means of which we interpret an unknown language?'⁶ Does not the meaning of linguistic impressions lie in the way the expressions are used? Is there a need for yet another system of reference — in addition to the rules for the use of words — in order to understand a language?

In the *Tractatus*, Wittgenstein was definitely of the opinion that it is possible to provide a general form of description: 'the general sentence-form'. Nothing less was meant by 'general sentence-form' than the 'essence of a proposition' (TLP 5.471). This finds its strongest expression in the statement of proposition 5.4711: 'To give the essence of a proposition means to give the essence of all description, and thus the essence of the world.' Not that Wittgenstein was about to give up his *idée fixe* that the essence of the world is made accessible by the discovery of the true nature of its description. Also in his later investigations, he held to the idea that grammar is what makes essence accessible. However, it was no longer the theory of the proposition that was to be burdened with the achievement of this task. In the place of the theory of the proposition, a set of interconnected concepts was introduced, among whose key members were: the use of expressions, the *language game*, in which words or signs find their usage, *rules* of usage; and *common judgements* and *common ways of acting*. But this set of concepts ought not, and cannot, be treated from within the framework of a system which the explanation of linguistic expressions were meant to serve.

Wittgenstein's clear dismissal of the need to *explain* the phenomena of language has misled many philosophers into believing that his position on the character of the treatment of philosophical problems is uninsightful and they have rejected it as a result, while regarding the key concepts as utterly comprehensible and acceptable. When one knows one's way around on the Wittgenstein conceptual map of the art of describing language games, one also knows one's way around in what Wittgenstein says about the nature of philosophical questions. Here I can merely touch on this issue. Just so much is brought to mind, when he states in the *Philosophical investigations*:

> Grammar does not tell us how language must be constructed in order to fulfil its purpose, in order to have such-and-such an effect on human beings. It only describes and in no way explains the use of signs. (PI §496)

And so he only repeats here what he emphasises at many points elsewhere, namely that descriptions of the actual use of expressions provide neither a foundation nor a (causal) explanation of linguistic behaviour. Similarly it does not provide a normative evaluation of the use of language, or an ideal that would serve as a norm. The task of grammar is much more to investigate the question (among others) of *whether* the meaning of linguistic expressions could or could not be given a causal explanation. Accordingly, the description is a phenomenological one to the extent that it concerns the *form of representation* itself:

> The concept of a perspicuous representation is of fundamental significance for us. It earmarks the form of account we give, the way we look at things. (PI§122)

Grammer is lacking in perspicuity, and 'perspicuity' basically means nothing other than an understanding which consists in seeing connections.[7] It has been thought that a Kantian idea is at work here, from the *Tractatus* to Wittgenstein's later work, namely, that consciousness or understanding *gives form to* nature.[8] The attempt to interpret Wittgenstein as a transcendental philosopher of Kantian derivation appears to me to be unconvincing from the outset. It is beginning to seem more and more appropriate to see this alleged Kantian connection as an echo of Spengler's influence. Wittgenstein had to master the difficulties of a realistic semantics; the conception of a contextual theory of language could only have contributed to this endeavour, as long as it did not bring with it the burden of an idealistic dependence upon the subject. The similarities between comparable forms and objects are of course speculative, but they have their basis in universal properties. For this reason I hold it worthwhile to set out this position, because through it we can grasp the role played by the common behaviour of mankind in the construction of a linguistic phenomenology, and in the grounding of pragmatics.[9]

It is known that Wittgenstein tried to offset the obvious weaknesses of a realistic semantics by applying a pragmatic-operationalist conception. The accomplishments of language are not realised in virtue of a unified schema, which could be represented by the concept of the *aliquid-pro-quo-stat*. What is accomplished in language is not to be drawn from or attributed to one scheme alone. In particular, the key concept in semantics, that of meaning, ought not to be determined on the model of the name and the object named, but in accord with its multifarious function, by its *use* in the language. The notion of a language game is introduced as a basic concept, a mirage-like concept that contains many meanings within itself. As has long been known, at least *four* different meanings of the term 'language game' must be distinguished: first, primitive languages and models of language; second, speech acts like naming, asking, describing and commanding; third, activities like play-acting, singing a roundelay, and gossiping; and fourth, the whole of language: 'language and the actions into which it is woven'.[10] As little as a historical perspective is usually associated with Wittgenstein's method the concept of a language game is essentially linked with the idea of change: 'new types of language, new language games, as we may say, come into existence, and others become obsolete and get forgotten'.[11] Language games must then be regarded as variable, mutable, and transitory. More precisely, one ought to say that human societies and communities invent, maintain and even forget language games. This has much to do with usage. For naturally, an individual can institute such a thing only in exceptional cases, and then only under the condition that it is accepted by the community; that is, accepted as social practice. If one now describes an actual (or conceivable) language game, it is most important that one 'really' describes 'something'.[12] But, what is to count as *real*? Certainly not an abstract reality, nor a theory to be stretched out in front of the oncoming train of facts: 'The essence of the language game is a practical method (a way of acting), not speculation, not empty talk.'[13] If we should want to clarify the sense of the concept of a cause, then it makes no sense to doubt the possibility of ever discovering or identifying a cause. We must have courage and begin with a deed, that is, with a speech act, which gives us a raw form.

> The game of 'looking for the cause', *consists* above all in a certain practice a certain method ... First there must be firm hard stone for building, and the blocks are laid rough-hewn one on another. *Afterwards* it's certainly important that the stones can be trimmed, that it's not *too* hard. The primitive form of the language game is certainty, not uncertainty. For uncertainty could never lead to action ... I want to say: it is characteristic of our language that the foundation on which it grows consists in steady ways of living, regular ways of acting.
>
> Its function is determined *above all* by action, which it accompanies.
>
> We have an idea of which ways of living are primitive, and which could only have developed out of these. We believe that the simplest plough existed before the complicated one. The simple form (that is the prototype) of the cause-effect game is determining the cause, not doubting.[14]

In this text, the following comes across as most striking: that the forms of life — a notion that is mentioned only five times in the *Investigations* — can be understood by looking at two features, one given by the concept of a pure action, and the other by the concept of its regularity. More important still, it appears to me, is the gradation of the concept of the form of life, which presupposes an order of an ever more complex, and thereby, involved, pyramid of forms of life, whose basis is provided by the primitive form. The primitive or simplest form is the *prototype*.

This concept of the prototype is, I believe, one of the substantive ideas that Wittgenstein took from Spengler's work. With this move he is, however, quite clearly reaching back to Goethe, and not to Kant. Spengler used both Goethe's expression 'proto-phenomenon' (*Urphänomen*) as well as the term *Ursymbol* (original symbol), in order to designate the entity in which the physiognomy of the historical form of life finds its ideal and potential origin. 'A proto-phenomenon', Spengler writes, 'is that in which the idea of becoming appears purely, right before our eyes.'[15] Spengler refers here to Goethe's studies in morphology, to the development of the *os inter maxillare* in vertebrates, to the 'leaf as the prototype of all plant organs', and to the 'metamorphosis of plants as the prototype of all organic Becoming'.[16] But culture is the proto-phenomenon in general: 'Every culture already possesses a completely individual way of seeing or knowing the world as *nature*, or, what is the same, each culture has its own peculiar nature, which no other kind of person can possess in quite the same shape.'[17] It does not seem to me to be at all true that, as von Wright proposed in commenting on *Culture and value* (*Vermischte Bemerkungen*), Wittgenstein took 'only' the concept of 'family resemblance' from Spengler's morphological remarks. It is advisable to proceed from the assumption that Wittgenstein discovered one of the methods related to his own investigations in *The Decline of the West*, and not only a graphic portrait of comparative morphology. And naturally, not only a method, but also a theory, along with all of the examples that such a theory brings with it. As he had done with other authors, Wittgenstein refers again and again to the work that he'd once grappled with, always making it say something new. (I do not speak here of Spengler's general outlook and the echoes that this might have occasioned in Wittgenstein.[18])

The concepts of the prototype and of the proto-phenomenon play, through diverse means, a role in Wittgenstein's investigations that cannot be overlooked, and whose content as well as methodological significance can be shown. Their most striking and well-known role is that of suspending explanatory investigations by merely pointing to the fact that a certain language game is being played. Let us take as an example the report of a past intention. What is the case when one reports what he *wanted* to say or do? One possible way of clarifying (and exemplifying) what obtains in such a case lies in imagining to oneself a concrete situation — in a sense, a 'natural fact'.

> Suppose we expressed the fact that a man had an intention by saying 'He as it were said to himself "I will"' — That is the picture. And now I want to know: how does one employ the expression 'as it were to say something to oneself'? For it does not mean: to say something to oneself. (PI §658)

That we wanted to say something at an earlier point in time, and didn't say it, is illuminated by looking at the simple form that is given expression in the example 'as it were to say something to oneself'. Considering the grammar of the use of this expression, it becomes clear that what we are concerned with here is an expression that is related to other expressions. However, in order to see this kinship, one must first look at the *actual* language game: 'Look at the language game as the *primary* thing.' If one wants to query or analyse the claim that psychological or inner experiences and reflection upon them are essential or inalienable to the process of determining the meaning of expressions, then it is appropriate first of all to consider the question: in which *surroundings* is something *in fact* said, and in which surroundings could it be said?[19]

> Ask not: 'What goes on in us when we are certain that...' — but: How is the 'certainty that this is the case' manifested in human action? (PI II xi, p. 225)

> Our mistake is to look for an explanation where we ought to look at what happens as a 'proto-phenomenon'. That is, where we ought to have said: *this language game is played.* (PI §654)

Since Wittgenstein invited us to regard the actual language game as primary and rejects as absurd the idea that it is possible to 'get beneath' the language game, it could look as though he wanted — like Spengler — to provide a comparative morphology of linguistic actions. The appearance is not deceptive, in so far as we understand this to be a question of *approach*.

The language game as an object of comparison should not be confused with objects of observation or facts of nature. To make this mistake leads to what Wittgenstein refers to as 'dogmatism',

and he reproaches Spengler for furthering such a dogmatic interpretation. To take the language game as an object of comparison,
that is, as a proto-form or measure, is not to take it as a standard
'to which everything has to conform' but as 'the principle determining the form of one's reflections'.[20] The concept of a 'form of
reflection' (*Betrachtungsform*) is an enticing but misleading one. It
leads one to the discovery of a 'fruitful new aspect' according to
which a reflection is taken as a principle that is given to us *a priori*,
like the Kantian forms of the intuition. But this interpretation
overlooks that what we are concerned with here is a *methodological*
device, not a theoretical or dogmatic one. In 1940 Wittgenstein
wrote: 'One of the most important methods I use is to imagine a
historical development for our ideas different from what actually
occurred. If we do this we see the problem from a completely new
angle.'[21]

Were the various language games that Wittgenstein investigates nothing other than thought experiments — like languages
composed only of commands, reports, or questions — then the
forms of life which, one imagines, are communicated by language
games would be nothing more than products of the imagination,
for whose application there could be no other criterion than the
current form of reflection. It is the understanding of interconnections that can be formed and altered by the form of representation. Thus Wittgenstein compares, in the second part of the
Investigations as well as at several other points in his work, the way
in which we form concepts with a style of painting. Such a
comparison also makes it apparent that talk of ' "right" concepts'
can only come up when one brings them into relation with
certain 'natural facts'. For if one imagines other facts of nature, it
immediately becomes clear that there is no necessity about the
usage of linguistic expressions. This appears to move counter to
the rule-bound character of language games, with all of their
internal relations. However, appearances deceive here, as so
often. The arbitrariness that we seem to approach here in
suggesting that the rules of the language are not valid in themselves, but are valid only for those who play or recognise a
language game, is an arbitrariness that is limited 'from inside' by
the fact of following rules, and 'from outside' by the form of life.
When we think or say that 'everything could be other than it is',
when we discover or invent anomalies, then the general *form of
representation*, with the help of which we reflect upon things, and
the uses of words, begins to appear to vacillate. And in the place

of the one system there may enter another, just as the form (that is, the meaning internal to a system) may change when the rules are changed. What, then, could lend some hold to our form of representation? Before looking into the answer (which inspired this paper) to this question, one sort of possible response should be put by the wayside — namely, the sort of self-affirmation that is really nothing other than a circular argument. If, that is, the language game does not foresee the possibility that things could be other than they are, then one cannot argue for the 'rightness' of the language game by pointing to the exclusion of such a possibility. Naturally, we know that there are other language games: 'an education completely different from our own could also be the basis of completely different concepts' (Z §387). 'For life would go on in a different way here' (Z §388).

Some have thought it warranted to interpret Wittgenstein's position on language games and forms of life as the categorial framework of a relativistic perspectivism, a framework that, to an extent, anticipates an epistemological perspectivism, if it doesn't already begin to provide one.[22] This has, among other consequences, the baleful consequence that, with the suspension of the question of truth, every linguistic form for which the status of a form of life is requested or proposed is thereby justified. Such an attempt at lending sanction to any and, as I shall argue, every sort of speculation and prattle nonetheless runs aground on Wittgenstein's foundationalism.

We have already determined that the language game does not take place in a vacuum. The network of all our actions is also a network of social relationships. And the social reality of this network shows itself in the fact that a change in conceptual scheme brings with it a change in the form of life. Nonetheless one should regard such a change — according to Wittgenstein — not as causally determined, for the simple reason that conceptual relations cannot be described within the conceptual scheme of cause and effect. To be sure, it is in the field of historical experience that the rootedness of forms of life in traditions presents itself most strikingly. When we reflect upon the emergence and passing of events — that is, when we regard events diachronically — then we also grasp the changes undergone by forms of life, and their deep attachments to the language. Indeed literally, the institutional aspect of language becomes obvious as we realise that we are members of a tradition that permeates all that we do and say. The acquisition of language itself follows the path of custom and habit, of rules and regularities: 'The regularity of our language permeates our lives.'[23] And so the thought arises that whoever can get 'behind' the rules — whoever can, so to speak, glimpse the reverse side of the mirror — could also grasp the form of life in its essence. But Wittgenstein eschews the search for a transcendental route: 'No one can push beyond the rules, because there is no Beyond.'[24]

Is this just another way of saying that the rules themselves provide a final justification for our language games? Are they the foundation we seek? Not at all: Wittgenstein's praxeological foundationalism vacillates in stating what lies at the basis of the language game; what, therefore, it is supposed to ground. For one, it surely includes the regularity of custom: of the activities and rules of action given by the traditions of society. Thus he once wrote, in the *Lectures and conversations on aesthetics*:

> To a language game belongs an entire culture. If one wants to describe musical taste, one must include in the description whether children give concerts, whether women or only men do this, etc. In aristocratic Viennese circles people had taste, then came the bourgeois circles, where the women went into choirs, and so on. This is an example of tradition in music.[25]

Now such a culture can also be regarded — and this is a Splenglerian thought — from a historic-typological point of view; it can be represented in its historical evolution. However, 'historical evolution, or the explanation as a hypothesis about evolution, is only *one* kind of compilation of the data — their synopsis'. It directs our attention to the effectiveness of tradition, to the totality of rules and practices which pervade our lives. From it, we gain not only our picture of the world, but also the conviction that it is not necessary to question beyond the forms of life embedded in it. If this is so, then the form of life represents a foundation only in so far as the network of convictions inside of which we carry on must rest upon it. About one such picture of the world, Wittgenstein writes:

> But I did not get my picture of the world by satisfying myself of its correctness; nor do I have it because I am satisfied of its correctness. No: it is the inherited background against which I distinguish between true and false. (OC §94)

In so far as this inherited background changes, our judgements and forms of life change also. Nonetheless, to inquire after the ground and justification of a form of life *within* that form of life is to direct a question at a void; it is to pose a senseless question.

> You must bear in mind that the language game is so to say something unpredictable. I mean: it is not based on grounds. It is not reasonable (or unreasonable).
> It is there — like our life. (OC §559)

Of course, Wittgenstein's praxeological foundationalism provides another, 'deeper' way in which to pose the question of ultimate foundations. Wittgenstein distinguishes between the historical, genetic explanation that has been the subject of discussion thus far, and a synchronic representation that allows us 'to see the data in their relations to each other and to bring them together in a general picture, without making it in the form of a hypothesis about evolution through time'.[26]

This synchronic, non-historical version of Wittgenstein's praxeological foundationalism breaks through where Wittgenstein attempts to give an epistemic justification for linguistic action in general. For the frame of reference by means of which every language is to be interpreted cannot be yet another language. Also, it cannot be the case that the common behaviour of mankind is being introduced to make the distinction between one picture of the world and another, for obviously, diachronic-historical knowledge has already shown that there have been different pictures of the world and thus that there can be such. And to the extent that pictures of the world and forms of life are bound up with — Wittgenstein would say 'coupled with' — each other, the frame of reference can inhere in, or be identical with, neither the picture of the world nor the form of life. Rather, we must look upon 'the common behaviour of mankind' as a ground that transcends the picture of the world, a ground upon which we — from the perspective of different forms of representation — *distinguish* pictures of the world and forms of life.

I do not want to claim that Wittgenstein resolved all of these deep difficulties. Far too much remains unclear. Nevertheless, it is possible to determine his main thesis. For naturally, the ground that transcends the picture of the world is, to Wittgenstein's understanding, not a transcendental condition but is rather, quite straightforwardly, a fact of experience: 'It is a fact of experience that human beings alter their concepts, exchange them for others when they learn new facts.'[27] It is *facts* which sometimes, though not always, lead to new concepts. But it is not just any fact, but such facts as bring us into agreement in our judgements and in our actions; such facts as serve as the basis of our understanding. If there were no agreement in action, there would also be no common concepts, and therefore no concepts at all. For the individualistic-sensualistic solution, that of a private conceptual scheme, remains out of the question for logical reasons, just as the construction of a society or a custom for a single individual would not be possible. In some passages, Wittgenstein quite clearly takes the offensive against the tendency to read a transcendental condition out of indications of an actual, factual conformity among human beings. Actually, he wants only to say 'that a language game is only possible if one trusts something'. At the same time, however, he emphasises that he is not saying 'if one can trust something'.[28]

So also, by way of the example of colour concepts:

'If humans were not in general agreed about the colours of things, if undetermined cases were not exceptional, then our concept of colour could not exist.' No — our concept *would* not exist.[29]

And also in the case of knowledge:

In order to make a mistake, a man must already judge in conformity with mankind.[30]

The fact that one takes over forms and concepts is not itself conditioned by forms and concepts, but by modes of acting. One could call these ways of acting 'ultimate conditions'. Does this mean that it is not possible to inquire after further justifications? In a certain sense, yes. But this sense is not a logical one; it is rather a *praxeological* one. The nature of the agreement is not such that it itself *determines* that we express ourselves *within* the language and communicate with each other *through* it. It is much more the case that *communicative action itself is the condition of agreement.* To the extent that it concerns judgements of truth or falsity, agreement in convictions and beliefs presupposes a common field of actions which cannot itself be called true or false (expressed in a different way: in which the concepts of truth and falsity are not applicable). If the true is what is grounded, then the ground is not *true*, nor yet false. (OC §205)

It is also true that it is impossible to find a further ground or justification for the common behaviour of mankind, although it is the ultimate presupposition of all grounds and justifications.

> But the end [of grounds-giving] is not an ungrounded presupposition: it is an ungrounded way of acting.[31]

> I mean: this is simply what we *do*. This is use and custom among us, or a fact of our natural history.[32]

More precisely, it is therefore the case by this account that *facts of our natural history* ultimately constitute the foundation of human speech as well as of human knowledge, a foundation that is not itself to be grounded. In order to maintain the anti-essentialism on the level of language, the essentialist solution is shifted onto the level of the fact of completed actions. 'The common behaviour of mankind' can be thus understood as a somewhat obscure term designating a common essence of human beings, of their nature, to which we refer when we want to make comprehensible the fact that we are at all capable of coming to an understanding. This *nature*, about whose essential features Wittgenstein was so reluctant to speak, reveals the human being as social being, as *zoon politikon* — through the ages, another name for 'the common behaviour of mankind'.

Notes

1. Revised draft of my opening address at the Wittgenstein Symposium in Rome, 25-26 January 1979 (Topic: Language and Knowledge as Social Facts).

2. See also R. Haller, 'Ludwig Wittgenstein (1889-1951)', in *Neue Oesterreichische Biographie*, vol. XX (Vienna 1979), pp. 95-105. Cf. G. Janoska, 'Die Praxis in der Spätphilosophie Wittgensteins', *Manuskripte* 54 (1976), p. 85.

3. TLP 4.112.

4. PI I §133.

5. M. Schlick, 'The turning point in philosophy', in: A.J. Ayer (ed.), *Logical positivism* (New York, The Free Press, 1959), pp. 53-9; cf. Wittgen-

stein, 'For me on the contrary clarity, perspicuity are valuable in themselves' (1930), CV, p. 7e. Cf. also R. Rorty (ed.), *The linguistic turn*, (University of Chicago Press, Chicago, 1967).

6. L. Wittgenstein, ibid., 206.

7. Cf. ibid., 122.

8. Cf. P.M.S. Hacker, *Insight and illusion* (Oxford University Press, Oxford, 1972), pp. 25-32.

9. Cf. J.C. Nyiri, 'Wittgenstein's new traditionalism', in *Essays on Wittgenstein. In honour of G.H. von Wright. Acta Philosophica Fennica*, 28 (1976), pp. 503-12; G.H. von Wright, 'Wittgenstein in relation to his times', in E. Leinfellner, *et al.* (eds), *Wittgenstein and his impact upon contemporary thought. Proceedings of the 2nd International Wittgenstein Symposium* (Hölder-Pichler-Tempsky, Vienna, 1978), pp. 73-8.

10. Cf. PI I, §7 and §23-25.

11. Ibid., §23.

12. L. Wittgenstein, 'Cause and effect: intuitive awareness', ed. R. Rhees, *Philosophia*, VI (1976), p. 405.

13. Ibid., p. 405.

14. Ibid. pp. 20-1.

15. O. Spengler, *The decline of the west. Sketch of a morphology of the history of the world*, (Knopf, New York, 1926), p. 141 (German edn: tr.); cf. also L. Nelson, 'Spuk. Einweihung in die Wahrsagekunst O. Spenglers (1921)', in *Gesammelte Schriften*, vol. 3 (Meiner, Hamburg, 1974), pp. 349-552. Also in O. Neurath's *Anti-Spengler* (Munich 1921), one can recognise again his role as opponent of metaphysical ideal constructions. It is no wonder then that Wittgenstein was attracted to that in Spengler which Neurath rejected.

16. Spengler, ibid.

17. Ibid., p. 171.

18. Cf. Nyiri, 'Wittgenstein's new traditionalism', and von Wright, 'Wittgenstein in relation to his times'.

19. Cf. Wittgenstein's 'Remarks on Frazer's *Golden Bough*'.

20. CV p. 26e, 27e.

21. Ibid., p. 37e.

22. Cf. Chapter 7.

23. L. Wittgenstein, *Remarks on colour*, ed. G.E.M. Anscombe, (Blackwell, Oxford, 1977), p. 303.

24. PG IV, 24.

25. L. Wittgenstein, *Lectures and conversations on aesthetics, psychology and religious belief*, ed. Cyril Barrett, (University of California Press, Berkeley and Los Angeles, 1967), p. 29.

26. Wittgenstein, 'Remarks on Frazer's *Golden Bough*', p. 45 (German edn).

27. Z §352; cf. *Ludwig Wittgenstein and the Vienna Circle: conversations recorded by Friedrich Waismann*, trans. J. Schulte and B.F. McGuinness (Basil Blackwell, Oxford, 1967), p. 162f. (German edn) 'Wir können nur eines in der Welt postulieren, das ist unsere Ausdrucksweise. Das Verhalten der Tatsachen können wir nicht postulieren.' ('We can only postulate one thing in the world, that is, our means of expression. We cannot postulate the behaviour of facts.')

28. OC §509.
29. Z §351.
30. OC §156.
31. Ibid., §110.
32. RFM I, 63.

9

Form of Life or Forms of Life?
A Note on N. Garver's
'The Form of Life in Wittgenstein's
Philosophical Investigations'

In my opening address to the Wittgenstein Symposium in Rome I attempted to show why Wittgenstein could have regarded the 'common way behaviour of mankind' as the praxeological foundation of all language games, as the worldview-transcending ground on the basis of which we distinguish forms of life and worldviews.[1] It became clear that it is not the different forms of life, forms of action or types of action that are to be understood as subsumed under 'common behaviour of mankind', but rather something that might be called the nature of human existence, something that could best be illuminated by the classical notion of the *zoon politikon* — the human being as a social being. Against the background of the common behaviour of mankind, we interpret foreign and unknown languages, and draw the boundary between language and the non-human 'language' of bees and lions.

Newton Garver's reinterpretation of Wittgenstein's concept of the form of life, I believe, follows the same path. But his concern is to show that Wittgenstein's use of the term 'form of life' in the *Philosophical investigations* admits only of the singular and that there is no justification for its use in the plural. 'The Wittgensteinian forms of life are those of natural history: the cow-like, the fish-like, the dog-like, and the human.' And there is only one human form of life. Thus Garver comes to the conclusion that 'the human form of life may be identified with the common way of human acting'.[2]

As much as his comments on the common way of human acting as the basic form of human life may further our understanding of Wittgenstein's investigations, it seems to me that Garver's claim that Wittgenstein meant to speak of nothing more, in his scant five uses of the term 'form of life', than what he calls the common way of human acting, cannot be defended.

Max Black — among several others — studied these five occurrences of the term and gave an interpretation to each occurrence that diminishes the importance that has been attributed, by many philosophers, to the concept of a form of life. In particular, he challenges Malcolm's high estimation of the significance of this concept in Wittgenstein's work: 'The notion of "*Lebensform*" is not really very important for Wittgenstein.'[3] Black figures that we must admit to only three features of the expression 'form of life' that might well be definitive of Wittgenstein's usage, and thus of its meaning: firstly, that the mastery of a given sublanguage encompasses the possession of a particular form of life; secondly, that the term 'form of life' is applicable to activities that include the production of meaningful and comprehensible utterances; and thirdly, that forms of life contain language games as self-sufficient parts.

It seems to me that Black's article has succeeded in contributing a sketch of the bounds of the concept's meaning, and, together with this, has counteracted a tendency to overestimate the importance of the concept in Wittgenstein's thought. Were the interpretation that Garver proposes for the expression a correct one, then it would be wrong in every case to speak of a variety of forms of life. However, it could just as easily be held that there are *two* distinct *meanings* of *Lebensform* to be differentiated, just as we recognise several meanings for the term 'language game'. One meaning of *Lebensform* — which would admit of use only in the singular — would accordingly be the same as the meaning of Wittgenstein's expression 'the common way of human acting'; another would allow for several interpretations, all of them based on the hypothesis that there can be and are different forms of life, which, of necessity, also manifest themselves in actions and linguistic actions.

Garver evidently constructs his position on the basis of this differentiation. For naturally, one cannot deny that Wittgenstein himself used the expression 'form of life' in other contexts and in other writings, not only in the plural form, but also in an anthropological-sociocultural sense; such as when he says in the lectures on aesthetics: 'In order to achieve clarity on aesthetic expressions, one must describe forms of life.'[4] Or when he writes in the remarks on cause and effect that we have 'an idea of which of the forms of life are primitive, and which derive from these. We

believe that the simpler plough came before the more complicated one.'⁵

Perhaps the clearest counterexample to Garver's position
appears in *On certainty*. Wittgenstein distinguishes here between
two epistemic attitudes of certainty: a 'struggling' one, and a
'calm' one. The first has much to do with our presuppositions
and our being persuaded of something: we are persuaded that we
know something, but we lack a basis for the justification of that
which we think we know. Just as there are both assumptions that
can be questioned and indubitable assumptions, so it is possible
to distinguish these two types of certainty. One can, under certain
conditions, express calm certainty simply by asserting that one
knows that such-and-such is the case. This provides the background for Wittgenstein's remark that certainty is something
'animal-like', that is, beyond our intellectual need to give a
rational justification for it: 'Now I would like to regard this
certainty, [that is, the calm certainty expressed in the assertion 'I
know ...' R.H.] not as something akin to hastiness or superficiality, but as a form of life. (That is very badly expressed and
probably badly thought as well.)'⁶ This is, characteristically, the
same context as that which provides the background for the
problem raised in the decisive passage of the second part of the
Philosophical investigations, namely the question concerning the
epistemic attitude of certainty. One way of asking the question is:
'How is "the certainty that this is the case" manifested in human
action?'⁷ This is the question to which Wittgenstein always seems
to give different answers, because none seems to him to be a full
or satisfactory one. But why not? As far as I can see, it is because
he makes reference, in his inquiry into the justificational basis of
epistemic activity, to a background *given*, a reference which is
analogous to his appeal, in his explanation of our understanding
of words, to what is given by the language. People agree *in that*
they perform *actions* by using *language*. This is at the same time an
agreement about form — the 'form of life'. Wittgenstein brought
together his conception of what can meaningfully be said with the
idea of a logical space allowing shifts of perspective within it, a
game-space that includes and limits all that might possibly be
said at all. What is new in the later reflections and investigations
is that foundations are sought and found in the practices of everyday life, and the interconnections between habits, customs and
institutions on the one hand, and people's activities and views on
the other, become essential for the comprehension of linguistic

action. The understanding of linguistic action, like that of linguistic meaning, is only possible against the background of everyday practice, of human activity.

The well-known passage from the *Philosophical investigations* — 'What has to be accepted, the given, is — so one could say — *forms of life*'[8] — which Garver completely misunderstands, becomes clearer in this light. Confirmation for this can be found in Typescript No. 229 from the year 1946/7, which appears as Part I of the *Remarks on the philosophy of psychology*. It is found here in a context that brings the meaning of 'form of life', as it occurs in the passage from the *Investigations* mentioned above, into close connection with forms of activity that are also, in other passages, designated as language games. The 'back to the rough ground of language' is read here as a 'back to the facts' and *not* as the 'common behaviour of mankind' or — as Garver wanted to say — as '*the form of life*'.

It is just not the case that as long as we are speaking of natural laws, we must imagine '*always the same* form of life', as Garver has claimed. 'One of the most important methods I use is to imagine a historical development for our ideas different from what actually occurred. If we do this we see the problem from a completely new angle.'[9] In such circumstances, Wittgenstein believes, different aspects of a problem become visible. The 'historical development of our ideas' is itself, naturally, bound up with activity or what are called language games. It is for this reason that the context of the earlier passage sounds like the enumeration of language games in Part I of the *Investigations* and becomes expanded in the later passage, in connection with the question of mathematical certainty.

Originally — that is, after 1948 — the question was often raised as to whether and to what extent colours are something 'specific', which 'cannot be explained in virtue of anything else'. The principal question here is, then: 'What is achieved by description and report, at all?'[10] And the answer to the worry that colours, like sounds, are indefinable, reads:

> Instead of the elementary, the specific, the undefinable: the fact that we act in such-and-such a way, e.g. *punish* certain actions, *determine* the facts of a case, *give commands*, make reports, describe colors, take an interest in the feelings of others. The accepted, the given, are — one could say — the facts of life.[11]

Even in this passage, Wittgenstein gives the term 'form of life' as an alternative for the last expression. The expression 'facts of life' in this context, however, designates that which actually occurs, and these facts stand in opposition to what we want to say and to that towards which we are enticed, by the language and by our intellectual habits. It is Wittgenstein's own phenomenological approach which shifts his focus from explanation (of a causal way of thinking) to a merely descriptive one. If we are tempted to say that colours are something indefinable and specific, then his answer is: but we don't see red as something specific. 'Rather [we see] the *phenomena* that are demarcated by the language game with the word "red".'[12]

I believe that enough has been said to be able to declare that the majority of occurrences of the term 'form of life' correspond to the majority of the occurrences of the term 'fact', and that there is no good reason to insist that Wittgenstein really wanted to use the singular expression where the plural stands.

It remains to say a few words concerning the origin of this expression. Unfortunately, Janik and Toulmin[13] have named Eduard Spranger as one of the principal sources — perhaps even the principal source — of the use of the term by Wittgenstein. This is obviously false. Already in 1911, W. Fred had published a collection of articles under the title *Lebensformen*, which was reviewed by Hugo von Hofmannsthal in the same year. In this discussion we read:

> No one wants to give much weight to forms, and yet every-thing we do adheres to and depends upon forms. Through forms, the multifarious hangs together fairly well, and presents itself as a whole. Forms are here forms of life (*Lebensformen*), old and yet new; they proceed in stops and starts, yet express the essential about the relations, and say without words what no one would agree to if said with words and concepts.[14]

It would not be so far-fetched to recall here the 'agreement' that Wittgenstein speaks of in §241 of the *Philisophical investigations*. In his collection of articles, which concerns alternative values and whose range of topics includes society and sociability, fashion, love and society, sports and games, the art of cuisine, and the art of travelling, Fred (Alfred Wechsler's pseudonym) has given precedence to a chapter entitled 'Form of life and forms of life'.

There he poses the question of the extent to which the individual, who seeks to find and construct his own form of life, is able to free himself from the forms that comprise society and culture. He believes that the individual is indeed at liberty to choose his own form of life, and ought to do so, but that the totality of forms of life — 'all forms are languages' — or that which is also called the culture of a society, cannot be shaped and created by individuals.[15]

When one says that to imagine a language is to imagine a form of life (PI §19), it is included in and implied by this statement that there are a number of forms of life and not just one. And just as surely this does not mean the cow-like, fish-like, dog-like and so on, but rather other human behaviour, other societies, real or imagined. In these Wittgenstein seeks the praxeological foundation for the understanding of linguistic actions. For this reason he could say that his examples for simple language games are not *theoretical* concepts, or, so to speak, idealised versions of common notions, but 'poles' which indicate the endpoints of possible gradations. This understanding of his own position shows, on the level of philosophical reflection, that one of the objections that are close at hand, namely, that the simple language games could not mirror the complexity of the actual, is an empty one. From the 'physiognomic' perspective, the discovery of which Wittgenstein shares with Spengler and Goethe, the whole Gestalt must always be considered in the interpretation of a particular. For this reason, it appears simply unreasonable to claim that the alternative forms of life that Wittgenstein spoke of don't also express differences between actual forms of life, or express them at least in many cases. It does not strike me as very persuasive when Garver does not admit one of the five passages as one of the 'principal sources' only because of the fact that it contradicts his own interpretation. When Wittgenstein considers the question of what a society of the 'feeble-minded', a society, that is, 'that never played many of our customary language games' would look like, he designates this question as an *important* one. And in his answer there appears an expressive device he often uses and which I mentioned earlier, namely, that of placing a phenomenon in another context, another order.

One imagines the feeble-minded under the aspect of the degenerate, the essentially incomplete, as it were in tatters. And so under that of disorder instead of a more primitive order (which would be a far more fruitful way of looking at them).

We just don't see a *society* of such people.[16]

Thus Wittgenstein frequently uses examples involving groups, tribes, and societies that behave differently from the way we do here and now, and maintain customs, practices and distinctions that are not familiar to us. That there are societies which use scales and concepts of colour different from ours — an example Wittgenstein uses often — is an empirically well-established fact.

Enough said; I wanted only to draw attention to an empirical inclination in the outlook of this great philosopher, an inclination that is often overlooked. Also, I had wanted to indicate a number of misunderstandings concerning the plural form of a key term in Wittgenstein's thought.

If I may allow myself a closing remark, I would like to point out that three years after the appearance of W. Fred's book on *Forms of life*, there appeared a collection of essays by a Viennese poet, one of the early contributors to *Die Fackel*, and a friend of Paul Ernst, Otto Stoessl: *Lebensform und Dichtungsform* ('Form of life and poetic form'). In the essay by the same title, the three prototypical forms of poetry — lyric, dramatic, and epic — are projected back onto the forms of life that arise among humans:

> In poetry, the poetic grows and ripens out of the form of life, and each contains after its own manner, in its language and with its means of representation, the whole of the world, as this is contained in the individual person, in the family, and in the state as a whole.[17]

And for Stoessl the individual in his individuation corresponds to the 'destined men', the lyrical form — 'The language is the only measure of things.' To the dramatic form, there corresponds the family 'as first bonding of opposing as well as related elements', and finally, corresponding to the epic form is 'the community, the tribe, the nation, the state, or however one wants to circumscribe the higher groupings of men into configuration determined by destiny'.[18]

Wittgenstein would not have adopted such ideas. But he shows, in measured clarity, that the concept of a form of life should be seen as a whole that corresponds to and underlies the literary art. And so the concept was used. To use it otherwise would have required special justification. But Wittgenstein offers no such thing. Why should we then impute one to him?

Notes

1. See Chapter 8.

2. N. Garver, 'Die Lebensform in Wittgenstein's *Philosophischen Untersuchungen*', *Grazer Philosophische Studien*, 21 (1984), pp. 33-54.

3. M. Black, 'Lebensform and Sprachspiel in Wittgenstein's later work', in E. Leinfellner, *et al.* (eds), *Wittgenstein and his impact on contemporary philosophy. Proceedings of the 2nd international Wittgenstein symposium.* (Hölder-Pichler-Tempsky, Vienna, 1978), pp. 325-31.

4. L. Wittgenstein, *Lectures and conversations on aesthetics, psychology and religious belief*, ed. C. Barrett (University of California Press, Berkeley and Los Angeles, 1967).

5. L. Wittgenstein, 'Cause and effect: intuitive awareness', ed. R. Rhees, *Philosophia*, 6 (1976), p. 420.

6. OC §358; Cf. §§356, 357, 359.

7. PI II XI, p. 225e.

8. Ibid., p. 226e.

9. CV p. 37e.

10. L. Wittgenstein, *Remarks on the philosophy of psychology*, I, ed. G.E.M. Anscombe and G.H. von Wright (Blackwell, Oxford, 1980), §§619-28.

11. Ibid., I §630.

12. Ibid., I §619.

13. A. Janik and S. Toulmin, *Wittgenstein's Vienna*, (Simon and Schuster, New York, 1973), pp. 230ff.

14. H. von Hofmannsthal, '"Lebensformen" von W. Fred', in his *Gesammelte Werke, Reden und Aufsätze I (1891-1913)*, (Suhrkamp, Frankfurt, 1979), p. 400.

15. W. Fred, *Lebensformen*, 3rd edn, (Munich-Leipzig, n.d.), p. 18ff. (The same author, by the way, is responsible for the first extensive study of the commodity character of literature: W. Fred, *Literature als Ware*, (Oesterheld, Berlin, 1911). In his book *Architektur als Symbol*, ('Architecture as symbol') (Schroll, Vienna, 1931), Josef Frank uses the expression 'Lebensform' to contrast life in Metropolis, Philemon and Baucis, and to thereby clarify the basic principles of modern architecture. Moritz Schlick notes something similar. 'There are different forms of life. The narrowminded and uneducated tend to display contempt for those forms to which they do not belong.' In M. Schlick, *Aphorismen*, ed. B. Hardy Schlick (Vienna, 1962), p. 39.

16. Z §372; cf. §§371, 373-381. See also: Wittgenstein, *Remarks on the philosophy of psychology* I, §§645, 646.

17. O. Stoessl, *Lebensform und Dichtungsform. Essays.* (Munich-Leipzig, 1914), p. 8, cf. p. 23.

18. Ibid., p. 7.

Bibliography

Albert, H. (1968) *Traktat über kritische Vernunft*, J.C.B. Mohr, Tübingen

Anscombe, G.E.M. (1959) *An introduction to Wittgenstein's Tractatus*, Hutchinson, London

—— (1976) 'The question of linguistic idealism', in *Essays on Wittgenstein in honor of G.H. von Wright, Acta Philosophica Fennica*, 28, pp. 209ff.

Ayer, A.J. (ed.) (1959) *Logical positivism*, The Free Press, Glencoe, Ill.

Baker, G.P. (1979) 'Verehrung und Verkehrung: Waismann and Wittgenstein', in C.G. Luckhardt (ed.), *Wittgenstein, sources and perspectives*, Hassocks, Harvester, pp. 243-85

Bartley III, W.W. (1969) 'Sprach- und Wissenschaftstheorie als Werkzeuge einer Schulreform: Wittgenstein und Popper als österreichische Schullehrer', *Conceptus*, 3, pp. 6-22

—— (1973) *Wittgenstein*, J.B. Lippincott, Philadelphia-New York

Bergmann, H. (1909) *Das philosophische Werk Bernard Bolzanos*, M. Niemeyer, Halle

Black, M. (1939) 'Relations between logical positivism and the Cambridge School of Analysis', *Journal of Unified Science (Erkenntnis)* 8, pp. 24-35

—— (1970) 'Verifications and Wittgenstein's reflections on mathematics', in C.G. Granger (ed.), *Wittgenstein et le problème d'une philosophie de la science*, Edition du Centre National de la Recherche Scientifique, Paris, pp. 138-49

—— (1978) 'Lebensform und Sprachspiel in Wittgenstein's later work', in Leinfellner *et al.* (1978), pp. 325-31

Borgis, I. (1958) *Index zu Wittgensteins 'Tractatus logico-philosophicus' und Wittgenstein-Bibliographie*, Alber, Freiburg-Munich

Bouveresse, J. (1970) 'La notion de "Grammaire" chez le second Wittgenstein', in *Wittgenstein et le problème d'une philosophie de la science*, Edition du Centre National de la Recherche Scientifique, Paris, pp. 173-80

Bubner, R. (1968) 'Die Einheit in Wittgensteins Wandlungen', *Philosophische Rundschau*, 15, pp. 101-84

Carnap, R. (1934a) *The unity of science*, (engl. trans.), M. Black, London 1934. Originally published as 'Die physikalische Sprache als Universalsprache der Wissenschaft', in *Erkenntnis* 2 (1931-2)

—— (1934b) 'Theoretische Fragen und praktische Entscheidungen', *Natur und Geist* 2 (1934), repr. in H. Schleichert (ed.), *Logischer Empirismus — der Wiener Kreis*, Wilhelm Fink, Munich 1975

Carnap, R. (1934c, 1987) 'The task of the logic of science', in B. McGuinness (ed.), *Unified science*, Reidel, Dordrecht-Boston, pp. 46-66. Originally published as *Die Aufgaben der Wissenschaftslogik* (*Einheitswissenschaft, Schriften* 3) (ed. O. Neurath together with R. Carnap and H. Hahn), Gerold & Co., Vienna

—— (1937) *The logical syntax of language*, Kegan Paul Trench, Trubner & Co., London

—— (1967) *The logical structure of the world. Pseudoproblems in philosophy* (engl. trans. R.A. George), University of California Press, Berkeley (1969)

Cavell, S. (1962) 'The availability of Wittgenstein's later philosophy', *Philosophical Review*, 71, pp. 67-93

—— (1979) *The claim of reason*, Oxford University Press, New York

Chisholm, R.M. (1960a) 'Introduction' to Chisholm (1960b)

—— (ed.) (1960b) *Realism and the background of phenomenology*, Free Press, Glencoe, Ill.

Cloeren, H.-J. (ed.) (1972) *Philosophie als Sprachkritik im 19. Jahrhundert,* • (*textauswahl I*), Fromann-Holzboog, Stuttgart-Bad Cannstatt

Coffa, A. (1976) 'Carnap's Sprachauffassung circa 1932', in P. Asquith and F. Suppe (ed.), *PSA* (Proceedings of the Philosophy of Science Association)

Ehrenfels, Ch. von (1916) *Kosmologie*, Eugen Diederichs, Jena

Engel, S.M. (1971) *Wittgenstein's doctrine of the tyranny of language*, M. Nijhoff, The Hague

Essler, W. (ed.) (1985) *Epistemology, methodology, and philosophy of science* (Essays in Honor of Carl G. Hempel on the occasion of His 80th Birthday, January 8th, 1985), Reidel, Dordrecht-Boston (*Erkenntnis* 22)

Fann, K.T. (1969) *Wittgenstein's conception of philosophy*, Blackwell, Oxford

Feigl, H. (1974) 'Logical empiricism', in D. Runes (ed.), *Twentieth century philosophy*, New York

—— (1981) 'No pot of message', in R.S. Cohen (ed.), *Inquiries and provocations*, Reidel, Dordrecht

Findlay, J.N. (1963) *Meinong's theory of objects and values*, Clarendon Press, Oxford

Frank, J. (1931) *Architektur als Symbol*, Schroll, Vienna

Frank, Ph. (1941, 1961) *Science and its philosophy*, Collier, New York

Fred, W. (n.d.) *Lebensformen*, 3rd edn, Munich-Leipzig

—— (1911) *Literatur als Ware*, Oesterheld, Berlin

Gargani, A. (1982) 'Schlick and Wittgenstein: language and experience' in R. Haller (ed.), *Schlick und Neurath — Ein Symposion*, Rodopi, Amsterdam (*Grazer Philosophische Studien* 16/17), pp. 347-63, repr. in S.G. Shanker (ed.) (1984), vol. 1, pp. 275-86

Garver, N. (1984) 'Die Lebensform in Wittgensteins *Philosophischen Untersuchungen*', *Grazer Philosophische Studien*, 21, pp. 33-54

Gerber, G. (1884) *Die Sprache und das Erkennen*, R. Gaertner, Berlin

Bibliography

Griffin, J. (1964) *Wittgenstein's logical atomism*, Oxford University Press, Oxford

Grossman, R. (1974) *Meinong*, Routledge & Kegan Paul, London

Hacker, P.M.S. (1972) *Insight and illusion*, Oxford University Press, Oxford

Haller, R. (1959) 'Das "Zeichen" und die "Zeichenlehre" in der Philosophie der Neuzeit', *Archiv für Begriffsgeschichte*, 4, pp. 113-57

—— (1964) 'Das cartesische Dilemma', *Zeitschrift für philosophische Forschung*, 18, pp. 369-85

—— (1966a) 'Der Wiener Kreis und die analytische Philosophie', in F. Sauer (ed.), *Forschung und Fortschritt*, Graz, pp. 33-46, repr. in R. Haller (1979b), pp. 79-98

—— (1966b) 'Meinongs Gegenstandstheorie und Ontologie', *Journal of the History of Philosophy*, 4, pp. 313-24, repr. in R. Haller (1979b), pp. 49-65

—— (1968a) 'Ludwig Wittgenstein und die Österreichische Philosophie', *Wissenschaft und Weltbild*, 21, pp. 78-87, repr. in R. Haller (1979b), pp. 107-21

—— (1968b) 'Wittgenstein and Austrian philosophy', (eng. transl.) in J.C. Nyiri (1981), pp. 91-112

—— (1970) *Review* of: G.E. Moore, 'Eine Verteidigung des Common Sense', *Philosophischer Literaturanzeiger*, 23, pp. 55-7

—— (ed.) (1972) *Jenseits von Sein und Nichtsein. Beiträge zur Meinongforschung*, Akademische Druk- und Verlagsanstalt, Graz

—— (1974a) 'Concerning the so-called "Münchausen-Trilemma"', *Ratio*, 16, pp. 125-40

—— (1974b) 'Ludwig Wittgenstein', in W. Pollak (ed.), *Tausend Jahre Österreich. Eine biographische Chronik*, vol. 3, Jugend und Volk, Vienna-Munich, pp. 317-22

—— (1974c) 'Sprachkritik und Philosophie: Wittgenstein und Mauthner', in A. Doppler (ed.), *Die Sprachthematik in der österreichischen Literatur des 20. Jahrhunderts*, Institut für Österreichkunde, Vienna, repr. in R. Haller (1979b), pp. 123-40

—— (1977) *Review* of William Warren Bartley III, *Wittgenstein*, *Conceptus*, 27-9 (special issue), pp. 422-4

—— (1978) 'Philosophische Irrtümer und die Sprache', in E. Leinfellner *et al.* (ed.), pp. 298-302, repr. in R. Haller (1979b), pp. 123-40

Haller, R. (1979a) 'Ludwig Wittgenstein (1889-1951)', in *Neue Österreichische Biographie ab 1815. Große Österreicher*, vol. xx, Vienna, pp. 95-105

—— (1979b) *Studien zur österreichischen Philosophie.*, Rodopi, Amsterdam

—— (1979c) 'Über Otto Neurath', in R. Haller (1979b), pp. 99-105

—— (1981) 'Wittgenstein es Spengler', *Villagossag*, 22, pp. 313-15

—— (1982a) 'Das Neurath-Prinzip — Grundlagen und Folgerungen', in F. Stadler (ed.), *Arbeiterbildung in der Zwischenkriegszeit. Otto Neurath — Gerd Arntz*, Löcker, Vienna, repr. in R. Haller (1986), pp. 108-24

—— (1982b) 'New light on the Vienna Circle', Monist, 165, pp. 25-37

—— (ed.) (1982c) *Schlick und Neurath — Ein Symposion*, Rodopi, Amsterdam (*Grazer Philosophische Studien* 16/17)

—— (1985a) 'Der erste Wiener Kreis', in W.K. Essler (ed.) (1985), pp. 341-59

—— (1985b) 'Philosophieren — Arbeit an einem selbst?', in P. Kruntorad (ed.), *A.E.I.O.U.*, Österreichischer Bundesverlag, Vienna, pp. 70ff

—— (1986) *Fragen zu Wittgenstein und Aufsätze zur Österreichischen Philosophie*, Rodopi, Amsterdam (*Studien zur Österreichischen Philosophie*, x)

Hamann, J.G. (1949-57) *Sämtliche Werke*, ed. J. Nadler, Herder, Vienna

Hartnack, J. (1965) *Wittgenstein and modern philosophy* (eng. trans. M. Evanston), Doubleday, New York

Hintikka, M. and Hintikka, J. (1986) *Investigating Wittgenstein*, Blackwell, Oxford

Hofmannsthal, H. von (1979) '"Lebensformen" von W. Fred', in Hofmannsthal, H. von, *Gesammelte Werke, Reden und Aufsätze I (1891-1913)*, Suhrkamp, Frankfurt

Janik, A. (1978) 'Wittgenstein and Weininger', in *Akten des 2. Int. Wittgenstein-Symposiums 29.8.-4.9.1977*, Hölder-Pichler-Tempsky, Vienna, repr. in Janik (1985), *Essays on Wittgenstein and Weininger*, Rodopi, Amsterdam (*Studien zur Österreichischen Philosophie*, ix)

—— (1985) *Essays on Wittgenstein and Weininger*, Rodopi, Amsterdam

—— and Toulmin, S. (1973) *Wittgenstein's Vienna*, Simon & Schuster, New York

Janoska, G. (1961) *Die sprachlichen Grundlagen der Philosophie*, Akademische Druck- und Verlagsanstalt, Graz

—— (1976) 'Die Praxis in der Philosophie Wittgensteins', *Manuskripte* 54

Joergensen, J. (1951) 'The development of logical positivism', in *International Encyclopedia of Unified Sciences*, 2/9, University of Chicago Press, Chicago

Johnston, W.M. (1972) *The Austrian mind. An intellectual and social history 1848-1938*, University of California Press, Berkeley-Los Angeles

Jones, E. (1945) 'Das Leben und das Werk von Sigmund Freud' *Journal of the History of Ideas* 6

Kamitz, R. (1973) *Positivismus. Befreiung vom Dogma*, Langen-Müller, Munich-Vienna

Kant, I. *Critique of pure reason* (1st edn 1781) (ed. and trans. N. Kemp Smith), Macmillan, London, 1929

—— *Prolegomena to any future metaphysics* (1783) (ed. L.W. Beck), Bobbs Merrill, New York, 1950

—— 'What is enlightenment?' (1784), in *Foundations of the metaphysics of morals* (eng. trans.) L.W. Beck), New York, 1950

Kastil, A. (1951) *Die Philosophie Franz Brentanos*, Francke, Bern

Kenny, A. (1973) *Wittgenstein*, Harvard University Press, Cambridge, Mass.

—— (1984) *The legacy of Wittgenstein*, Blackwell, Oxford

Kolakowski, L. (1968) *The alienation of reason. A history of positivist thought*, (eng. trans.) N. Guterman), Garden City, New York

Kraft, V. (1968) *Der Wiener Kreis. Der Ursprung des Neopositivismus. Ein Kapitel der jüngsten Philosophiegeschichte*, 2nd (enlarged) edn, Springer, Vienna.

———— *The Vienna Circle. The origin of neo-positivism*, (eng. trans. A. Pap), The Philosophical Library, New York

Kraus, O. (1919) *Franz Brentano*, Ch. Beck, Munich

Kripke, S. (1982) *Wittgenstein on rules and private language*, Blackwell, Oxford, Harvard University Press, Cambridge, Mass.

Lee, D. (ed.) (1980) *Wittgenstein lectures, Cambridge 1930-32*, Rowman & Littlefield, Totowa, N.J.

Leinfellner, E. (1968) 'Zur nominalistischen Begründung von Linguistik und Sprach-philosophie: Fritz Mauthner und Ludwig Wittgenstein', *Studium Generale*, 22, pp. 209-25

————, Leinfellner, W., Berghel, H., and Hübner, A. (eds) (1978), *Wittgenstein and his impact on contemporary thought* (Proceedings of the 2nd International Wittgenstein Symposium, Kirchberg am Wechsel, Austria, 1977), Hölder-Pichler-Tempsky, Vienna

Lenoci, M. (1972) *La teoria della connoscenza in Alexius Meinong*, Università Cattolica, Milan

LeRider, J. (1985) *Der Fall Otto Weininger. Wurzeln des Antifeminismus und Antisemitismus*, Löcker, Vienna

LeRider, J. and Leser, N. (eds) (1984) *Otto Weininger: Werk und Wirkung* (Quellen und Studien zur österreichischen Geistesgeschichte im 19. und 20. Jahrhundert, vol. 5), Österreichischer Bundesverlag, Vienna

Lorenz, K. (1970) *Elemente der Sprachkritik*, Suhrkamp, Frankfurt

Luckhardt, C.G. (ed.) (1979) *Wittgenstein, sources and perspectives*, Harvester, Hassocks

Malcolm, N. (1984) *Ludwig Wittgenstein. A memoir*, Oxford University Press, Oxford

———— (1986) *Nothing is hidden*, Blackwell, Oxford

Mauthner, F. (1901-2) *Beiträge zu einer Kritik der Sprache*, 3 vols, Cotta-Mundus, Stuttgart

———— (1910-11) *Wörterbuch der Philosophie*, 2 vols, G. Müller, Munich, repr. Diogenes, Zurich (1980)

———— (1913) 'Otto Friedrich Gruppe', *Die Zukunft* 85

———— (1922) 'Selbstdarstellung', in R. Schmidt (ed.), *Die Philosophie der Gegenwart in Selbstdarstellungen*, F. Meiner, Leipzig

Mises, R. von (1928) *Wahrscheinlichkeit, Statistik und Wahrheit* (Schriften zur wissenschaftlichen Weltauffassung, vol. 3), J. Springer, Vienna

Moore, G.E. (1924) 'A defence of common sense', in J.J. Muirhead (ed.), *Contemporary British philosophy* (2nd series), London, pp. 193-223; repr. in G.E. Moore (1959)

———— (1959) *Philosophical papers*, Routledge & Kegan Paul, London

Morscher, E. (1972) 'Von Bolzano zu Meinong: Zur Geschichte des logischen Realismus', in R. Haller (ed.) (1972)

Müller, A. (1967) *Ontologie in Wittgenstein's Tractatus*, Bouvier, Bonn

Mulligan, K. (1981) 'Philosophy, animality and justice: Kleist, Kafka, Weininger and Wittgenstein', in B. Smith (ed.), *Structure and Gestalt: philosophy and literature in Austria-Hungary and her successor states* (Linguistic and Literary Studies in Eastern Europe), John Benjamins B.V., Amsterdam

Nagel, E. (1936) 'Impressions and appraisals of analytic philosophy in Europe', *Journal of Philosophy*, 33, pp. 5-53, repr. in E. Nagel, *Logic without metaphysics and other essays in the philosophy of science*, The Free Press, Glencoe, Ill. (1956), pp. 191-246

——— (1961) *The structure of science. Problems in the logic of scientific explanation*, Harcourt, Brace & World, New York

Nelson, L. (1921) *Spuk. Einweihung in das Geheimnis der Wahrsagekunst Oswald Spenglers und sonnenklarer Beweis der Unwiderlegbarkeit seiner Weissagungen nebst Beiträgen zur Physiognomik des Zeitgeistes* (Eine Pfingstgabe für alle Adepten des metaphysischen Schauens), repr. in L. Nelson, *Gesammelte Schriften*, vol. 3, Meiner, Hamburg (1974), pp. 349-552

Neurath, O. (1921) *Anti-Spengler*, repr. in O. Neurath (1981), pp. 139-95

——— (1931) 'Soziologie im Physikalismus', in *Erkenntnis*, 21, pp. 393-431; repr. in O.Neurath (1981), pp. 533-62

——— (1959) 'Sociology and Physicalism' (eng. trans. M. Magnus and R. Raico), in A.J. Ayer (1959), pp. 282-371

——— (1931-2) 'Wege der wissenschaftlichen Weltauffassung', in *Erkenntnis*, 1, repr. in O. Neurath (1981), pp. 371-85

——— (1936) 'Physicalism and the investigation of knowledge', repr. in O. Neurath (1983)

——— (1971) *Empiricism and sociology*, (ed. M. Neurath and R.S. Cohen), Reidel, Dordrecht

——— (1981) *Gesammelte philosophische und methodologische Schriften*, (ed. R. Haller and H. Rutte), 2 vols, Hölder-Pichler-Tempsky, Vienna

——— (1983) *Philosophical papers 1913-1945*, (ed. R.S. Cohen and M. Neurath), Reidel, Dordrecht

Nyiri, J.C. (1976) 'Wittgenstein's new traditionalismus' *Essays on Wittgenstein in honor of G.H. von Wright*, in *Acta Philosophica Fennica*, 28, pp. 503-12

——— (1981) *Austrian philosophy. Texts and studies*, Philosophia, Munich

Pears, D. (1971) *Ludwig Wittgenstein*, Fontana, London

Pitcher, G. (1964) *The philosophy of Wittgenstein*, Prentice Hall, Englewood Cliffs, N.J.

Popper, K.R. (1959) *The logic of scientific discovery*, 2nd edn, Hutchinson, London

Rorty, R. (1967) *The linguistic turn*, The University of Chicago Press, Chicago

Runes, D. (ed.) (1974) *Twentieth century philosophy*, New York

Russell, B. (1921) *Analysis of mind*, Allen & Unwin, London

——— (1922) 'Introduction' to Wittgenstein, *Tractatus logico-philosophicus*, Humanities Press, Atlantic Highlands, 1974

——— (1973) *Essays in analysis*, (ed. D. Lackey), George Allen & Unwin, London

Rutte, H. (1982) 'Der Philosoph Otto Neurath', in F. Stadler (ed.), *Arbeiterbildung in der Zwischenkriegszeit*, Löcker, Vienna, pp. 70-8

Salamun, K. (1972) 'Das Philosophische Seminar an der Universität Graz', *Historisches Jahrbuch der Stadt Graz*, 5/6

Savigny, E. von (1969) *Die Philosophie der normalen Sprache*, Alber, Freiburg-Munich

Schilpp, P.A. (ed.) (1963) *The philosophy of Rudolf Carnap*, Library of Living Philosophers, Open Court, La Salle, Ill.

Bibliography

Schleichert, H. (ed.) (1975) *Logischer Empirismus — Der Wiener Kreis*, Wilhelm Fink, Munich

Schlick, M. (1930) 'The turning point in philosophy', in A.J. Ayer (ed.), *Logical positivism*, Free Press, New York (1959). Originally published in German as 'Die Wende der Philosophie', in *Erkenntnis*, 1, pp. 4-11

―――― (1934) 'On the foundation of knowledge', (engl. transl. P. Heath), in M. Schlick (1979), pp. 370-87. Originally published as 'Über das Fundament der Erkenntnis', in *Erkenntnis*, 4, pp. 79-99

―――― (1935) 'Facts and propositions', *Analysis*, 2, pp. 65-70, repr. in M. Schlick (1979), pp. 400-4

―――― (1962) *Aphorismen*, ed. B. Hardy Schlick, Vienna

―――― (1979) *Collected papers, vol. II (1925-1936)* (ed. H. Mulder and B.B.F. van der Velde-Schlick), Reidel, Dordrecht-Boston-London

Schmidt, R. (ed.) (1922) *Die Philosophie der Gegenwart in Selbstdarstellungen*, F. Meiner, Leipzig

Schmidt, D.J. (1971) *Philosophie als Sprachkritik im 19. Jahrhundert (Textauswahl II, Problemata)*, Froman und Holzboog, Stuttgart-Bad Cannstatt

Schulz, W. (1967) *Wittgenstein. Die Negation der Philosophie*, Neske, Pfullingen

Shanker, S.G. (1986) 'The significance of the *Tractatus*', in S.G. Shanker (ed.), *Ludwig Wittgenstein: critical assessments*, 4 vols, Croom Helm, London, vol. 1, pp. 16-33

Smith, B. (1985) 'Weininger and Wittgenstein' in B.F. McGuinness and A. Gargani (eds), *Wittgenstein and contemporary philosophy*, *Teoria*, v, pp. 227-57

Specht, E.K. (1963) 'Die sprachphilosophischen und ontologischen Grundlagen im Spätwerk Ludwig Wittgensteins', *Kant-Studien*, 84, Kölner Universitätsverlag, Cologne

Spengler, O. (1932) *The decline of the West. Sketch of a morphology of the history of the world*, Knopf, New York, 1926. Originally published as *Der Untergang des Abendlandes. Umrisse einer Morphologie der Weltgeschichte* (1918)

Stadler, F. (ed.) (1982) *Arbeiterbildung in der Zwischenkriegszeit. Otto Neurath — Gerd Arntz*, Löcker, Vienna-Munich

Stegmüller, W. (1965) 'Ludwig Wittgenstein als Ontologe, Isomorphietheoretiker, Transzendentalphilosoph und Konstruktivist', *Philosophische Rundschau*, 13, pp. 116-52

―――― (1969) *Hauptströmungen der Gegenwartsphilosophie*, 4th edn, Kröner, Stuttgart

Stenius, E. (1960) *Wittgenstein's Tractatus*, Basil Blackwell, Oxford

Stoessl, Otto (1914) *Lebensorm und Dichtungsform (Essays)*, Munich-Leipzig

Thiele, S. (1983) *Die Verwicklungen im Denken Wittgensteins*, Alber, Freiburg

Vuillemin, J. (1979) 'On Duhem's and Quine's theses', *Grazer Philosophische Studien*, 9, pp. 69-96

Waismann, F. (1965) *The principles of linguistic philosophy* (ed. R. Harré), Macmillan, London

―――― (1967) 'Theses', in L. Wittgenstein (1967c)

Wallner, F. (1983) *Die Grenzen der Sprache und der Erkenntnis (Philosophica*

1), Braumüller, Vienna

Weiler, G. (1955) 'On Fritz Mauthner's "Critique of Language"', *Mind*, 67, pp. 80-7

Weinberg, J.R. (1936) *An examination of logical positivism*, Routledge & Kegan Paul, London

Weininger, O. (1918) *Über die letzten Dinge*, Braumüller, Vienna-Leipzig

—— (1903) *Geschlecht und Charakter* Braumüller, Vienna-Leipzig

Wiggershaus, R. (ed.) (1975) *Sprachanalyse und Soziologie*, Suhrkamp, Frankfurt

Winter, E. (1969) 'Bernard Bolzano', in *Bernard Bolzano, Gesamtausgabe*, vol. 1, Fromann & Holzboog, Stuttgart

Wittgenstein, L. (1922) *Tractatus logico-philosophicus*, 'Introduction' by B. Russell. New edition (1961) (engl. trans) D.F. Pears and B.F. McGuinness), Routledge & Kegan Paul, London

—— (1953) *Philosophical investigations* (ed. G.E.M. Anscombe and R. Rhees, trans. G.E.M. Anscombe), Basil Blackwell, Oxford

—— (1956) *Remarks on the foundations of mathematics* (ed. G.H. von Wright, R. Rhees and G.E.M. Anscombe and trans. G.E.M. Anscombe), Basil Blackwell, Oxford. Revised edition MIT-Press, Cambridge, Mass. (1983)

—— (1958) *The blue and the brown books*, (ed. R. Rhee), Basil Blackwell, Oxford

—— (1961) *Notebooks 1914-1916* (ed. G.E.M. Anscombe and G.H. von Wright and trans. G.E.M. Anscombe), Basil Blackwell, Oxford

—— (1966) *Lectures and conversations on aesthetics, psychology and religious belief*, ed. C. Barrett, Basil Blackwell, Oxford

—— (1967a) *Zettel* (ed. G.E.M. Anscombe and G.H. von Wright and trans. G.E.M. Anscombe), Basil Blackwell, Oxford

—— (1967b) 'Bemerkungen zu Frazers *Golden Bough*', ed. R. Rhees, *Synthese*, 17

—— (1967c) *Ludwig Wittgenstein and the Vienna Circle: conversations recorded by Friedrich Waisman*, ed. B.F. McGuinness and trans. J. Schulte and B.F. McGuinness), Basil Blackwell, Oxford

—— (1969) *On certainty* (ed. G.E.M. Anscombe and G.H. von Wright) Basil Blackwell, Oxford

—— (1974) *Philosophical grammar* (ed. R. Rhees, and trans. A. Kenny), University of California Press, Los Angeles

—— (1975) *Philosophical remarks* (ed. R. Rhees and trans. G.E.M. Anscombe), Basil Blackwell, Oxford

—— (1976) 'Ursache und Wirkung: Intuitives Erfassen' (ed. R. Rhees), in *Philosophia* 6, pp. 409-24. 'Cause and Effect', (ed. R. Rhees and trans. P. Winch), *Philosophia*, 6, pp. 409-24

—— (1977) *Remarks on colour*, ed. G.E.M. Anscombe, Basil Blackwell, Oxford

—— (1980a) *Culture and value*, (ed. G.H. von Wright and trans. P. Winch), Basil Blackwell, Oxford-Chicago

—— (1980b) *Remarks on the philosophy of psychology* (vol. 1 ed. G.E.M. Anscombe and G.H. von Wright, vol. 2 ed. G.H. von Wright and Heikki Nyman), Basil Blackwell, Oxford

—— (1985) 'Geheime Tagebücher: der verschlüsselte Teil der

"Gmundener Notizbücher"', (ed. W. Baum), *Saber*, 6, pp. 475ff

Wright, G.H. von (1978) 'Wittgenstein in relation to his times', in Leinfellner *et al.* (eds), pp. 73-8

—— (1982) *Wittgenstein*, Basil Blackwell, Oxford

Wucherer-Huldenfeld, A. (1968) 'Sigmund Freud als Philosoph', *Wissenschaft und Weltbild*, 31

Wuchterl, K. (1969) *Struktur und Sprachspiel bei Wittgenstein*, Suhrkamp, Frankfurt

Index of Names

Index

147